Conversations Among Friends

Conversations Among Friends

Discussions about the Christian Faith

by

DENNIS TACKLEY

CONVERSATIONS AMONG FRIENDS

Discussions about the Christian Faith

by

DENNIS TACKLEY

12 The Waldrons
Thornford
Sherborne
Dorset
DT9 6PX

ISBN 0 9521347 0 5

Typeset, Printed and Bound by
Bourne Press, Bournemouth.

He wants not friends that hath Thy love,
And may converse and walk with Thee,
And with Thy saints here and above,
With whom for ever I must be.

Richard Baxter

Contents

The Thursday Group xi

Part One: Biblical Topics

1 Praying for Others 1
2 The Sea of Reeds 5
3 The Christmas Stories 9
4 The Humanity of Jesus 14
5 Jesus' Message 19
6 Sell Your Possessions 23
7 A Minister's Request 27
8 A Joint Venture 31
9 The Embarrassment of the Old Testament 36
10 Gospel Truth 41
11 An Interview with Paul 46
12 Misusing the Bible 51

Part Two: The Apostles' Creed

13 Believing in God 59
14 Undeserved Suffering 63
15 Was Jesus Divine? 67
16 An Alternative Story 71
17 The Atonement 75
18 The Resurrection 80
19 At God's Right Hand 85
20 The Day of Wrath 89
21 A Committee of Three? 93
22 One Church or Many? 98
23 The Life Everlasting 103
24 The Christian Pilgrimage 108

Foreword

This book makes a plea for deeper Christian fellowship. It shows how the doubts and questions of ordinary churchgoers can be faced in open and honest discussion. It stresses the importance of fellowship groups in the nurturing of Christian faith. In a word, it demonstrates one way in which the churches can set about the task of adult education - an area of church life which has only too often been neglected.

Many churchgoers do not find belief easy, and they may have harboured questions about the Christian faith they have never had the opportunity to ask. This book illustrates the value of the discussion group within which concerns can be shared, personal experiences recounted,and hard-won insights offered to others. There is a time for worship, but also a time for mutual encouragement which should be available to all who wish to follow the Christian way.

There is also an alarming gap between the world of the professional biblical scholar and theologian on the one hand, and the ordinary churchgoer on the other. This book shows how the gap can be bridged. It can be enjoyed as a 'good read', but it is primarily intended to encourage the development of fellowship groups in local churches. Its material can be used to initiate discussions, or to suggest possibilities to existing or potential group leaders.

We are in a decade of evangelism. This must involve the renewal of the churches themselves. There is no better way to achieve this than to tap the resources which already lie hidden in the minds and hearts of our existing church members. We must encourage open discussion and genuine sharing in which interested enquirers can join without embarrassment. This is not the same as *instruction*. Committed Christians are still seekers, pilgrims on the road to truth rather than purveyors of ready-made solutions. Faith must always seek greater understanding.

The Thursday Group

Let us suppose that in the new town of Barfield there is an ecumenical church, a joint venture in which the Anglican, Methodist, and United Reform Churches are all participating. The building is a fairly modern one, with a comfortable lounge next to a coffee bar. On the first Thursday evening of each month a discussion group meets to consider some aspect of the Christian faith.

All are made welcome, whether they are regular members of the congregation or not. After informal conversation over coffee, the meeting opens with a short prayer, a Bible reading, and a hymn. This ecumenical church - the Church of the Good Shepherd, to give it its official name - has decided to use the Methodist *Hymns and Psalms* (H&Ps) in its worship. Derek, the group's leader, sometimes chooses hymns by modern authors which are unfamiliar even to the Methodists present! The ensuing discussion usually lasts about half an hour, after which some time is spent in intercessory prayer.

The composition of the group remains fairly stable. Derek is a retired schoolmaster and a Methodist local preacher. He is ably assisted by Susan, an Anglican Reader who teaches religious education at the nearby comprehensive school. The most senior member of the group is Hilda, a sprightly septuagenarian who has held several church offices, first as a Congregationalist and then as a member of the URC. Frank has a responsible job in local government; he and his wife Gillian are Anglicans. Marion is a nurse at the local hospital, while Linda does secretarial work.

It should be mentioned that Andrew, the present minister at the church, has other commitments on Thursday evenings and is thus unable to attend these meetings. Four other members of the group deserve special mention. Harry helps with the church youth club but is without a job when these discussions begin; he moves away from Barfield after a few months. George, who appears in Part Two, is a business manager made redundant in the recession. Esther originally came from Barbados. Norman, another occasional member of the group, belongs to the Free Evangelical church in Barfield.

The members of the Thursday Group represent a variety of theological viewpoints. Derek would probably describe himself as a liberal, while Susan sometimes expresses quite radical views. At the other end of the spectrum, both Marion and Norman tend to be conservative in their outlook. Marion was converted years ago during a Billy Graham crusade; and Norman is accustomed to fundamentalist biblical teaching in his own church. Other members of the group are less easy to categorize, although it will be noticed that both Harry and George are somewhat sceptical in their attitude.

Yet, for most of the time at least, these who participate in the discussions agree to differ without ill-feeling. They all enjoy the fellowship they find at these meetings - and that includes those who prefer to remain silent for most of the time. All would readily admit to having learnt much from one another. They have grown in mutual understanding, and have sometimes found that their own beliefs have been modified in unexpected ways. Above all, they have grown more sure of their own faith and more confident in expressing their convictions.

Part One
Biblical Topics

1

Praying For Others

Preliminaries: Genesis 18 v.20-33 and 'O Christ, the Healer, we have come (H&Ps 395).

Derek: Today's theme is praying for others. What do we suppose happens when we do this? What is the most effective way to make intercessions? Let's start with the story we read from Genesis 18. It suggests that Abraham was able to change God's mind. God intended to destroy Sodom, but Abraham talked him out of it. Is this what we are trying to do when we pray for other people? Are we attempting to influence the way God acts? God is love. He has the best interests of all his children at heart. Do we really believe he's not going to act unless we urge him to? What do you think about this?

Gillian: I can't remember hearing that story before. It certainly gives the impression that Abraham was able to influence God. Can the story be explained in any other way?

Susan: Don't you think it was really Abraham who changed during the course of the story - not God? He came to realize that God was merciful. As a result of his prayer he came to understand God better. Isn't that the best way to interpret what happened?

Marion: I can't accept that. Surely we must take the story as it stands. God wants us to pray. He answers our prayers. That's what we mean by a personal relationship.

Derek: There's something in that. Perhaps we can regard our praying for others as a way of co-operating with God. I made a note somewhere of a quotation from St. Augustine . . . Here it is: 'Without God, we cannot; without us, God will not'.

Hilda: I do believe our prayers for others are answered. I've heard of some remarkable cases of healing brought about through prayer.

Harry: All the praying we did for Christine Burrows didn't do any good. She died of cancer just the same.

Hilda: We were all very distressed about that, Harry. But Christine was so calm and brave towards the end. And I know our prayers were a support to Gordon; he told me so afterwards.

Gillian: When you're in trouble, it's a great help to know people are praying for you. I know that from my own experience.

Derek: How do you think that kind of prayer works? Is it a form of telepathy? Are our minds or spirits all connected at some deep level?

Susan: That could be the case. There certainly seems to be a release of spiritual power. I remember a missionary saying once that the situation where she worked often began to improve at a particular time in the month. Then it dawned on her why.It was at the time when Sri Lanka was the subject of prayer in England.

Derek: You mean things changed when people using a prayer diary were concentrating on the church in Sri Lanka?

Susan: Yes. There was a more friendly attitude here, an offer of help there ... There was definitely a change of atmosphere, she said.

Derek: That's very interesting. Has anyone else seen how their prayers for others have been answered?

Harry: I don't know about prayers for others, but I've been praying for a job and nothing's turned up yet.

Marion: Perhaps you haven't been praying hard enough. The Bible tells us we've got to keep on asking until we get what we need.

Harry: I don't enjoy being out of work, you know. There just aren't the openings in my trade at the moment.

Derek: There are usually prayers for our national life in the Sunday service. Do you think general prayers of this kind can make a difference?

Marion: I don't see why not. Some glimmer of wisdom might get through to influence the decisions our leaders make.

Derek: What about praying for the peace of the world?

Hilda: I must admit, I find it easier to concentrate on particular people, on world rulers I can picture in my mind. Or at least on particular situations we have heard about in the news.

Susan: It's interesting you should say that. When I'm preparing a service I find the intercessions the hardest part to do. I'd welcome any suggestions you can make about that.

Derek: What do you all think? As members of a congregation, do you find general prayers helpful? Or is it better to concentrate on a few individuals, or on two or three particular situations?

Linda: It's helpful to mention people by name, especially when we're told what their needs are. I don't feel general prayers make much impact.

Gillian: That leaves out a lot of people - in the local hospitals, say - who have no-one to pray for them, and who lack the faith to pray for themselves.

Frank: When it comes to praying for the world, I like it when the preacher explains the circumstances in a particular country. Then we can pray with some understanding. It helps if we've read something about it, or seen it on television.

Susan: I was at a school service once when the clergyman spread the daily newspaper on the altar. Then he prayed for three or four situations that were in the headlines. I thought at the time how effective that was, but I've never seen it done since.

Linda: Coming back to praying for the sick, I think it helps if we can feel real sympathy for the people we're praying for. Don't you think *feeling* is important when we pray?

Derek: Some experts talk about 'empathy', the ability to put ourselves in the place of the person we're praying for and to feel something of what he or she is feeling.

Linda: That's easier to do in our private prayers, when we're not rushed for time.

Hilda: I agree we need to use our imagination. Many years ago I sometimes went to the City Temple to hear Leslie Weatherhead preach. In the time of intercession he used to introduce a few individual cases, and told us what was happening to the man or woman concerned. Then he invited us to concentrate in silence on each individual in turn. I'm sure prayers like that were very effective. There was a powerful atmosphere at that point in the service.

Gillian: I sometimes think the prayers of intercession are the most important part of a service. Here we are co-operating with God in his work of healing and restoration. Our prayers can be channels of grace. That's quite a responsibility!

Derek: Can we come back now to the question we began with? Is there any sense in which we are influencing what God does?

Susan: The way I see it, God is always offering himself to human beings. It's on the *human* side that barriers exist. Our prayers for others are helping to break those barriers down. We are standing with other human beings, inviting God's Spirit to enter more fully into their lives. That's the way we can influence what happens in the world.

Gillian: I can see what you mean, Susan, but I believe there must be more to it than that. The Bible often shows God listening to prayer and answering it. As Marion said, we have a personal relationship with God. He *is* influenced by our requests. That's what we mean by a personal God.

Frank: I don't like this picture of God sitting on his royal throne listening to various petitions, saying 'Yes' to some and 'No' to others. We need to move away from that kind of picture.

Hilda: I'm sure nobody here thinks like that, Frank. I don't understand why some of our prayers for others seem to remain unanswered. We cannot see the whole situation as God does. But we are urged to ask in Jesus' name, and we must trust that God uses our prayers in his own way.

Derek: We do seem to have a problem, though. We want to think of God always acting consistently, always seeking the well-being of all his children. Yet we also want to stress the personal nature of our relationship with him, a relationship involving request and response.

Susan: It's a basic issue in Christian theology. Is God above time and essentially unchanging, or is he involved in time and affected by his creation?

Derek: We're not going to be able to tackle that issue now. But we could consider more carefully how we think of God acting in the world. Perhaps next month we could take a biblical story which shows God acting directly in human affairs, and try to sort out the issues involved. Meanwhile, thank you all very much for your contributions to this evening's discussion.

Comment

Dr. Weatherhead once explained his practice at the City Temple in these terms: 'We do not imagine that we are persuading a reluctant God to intervene ... We rather believe that we are letting through God's healing, spiritual energies, which at that moment may be blocked on the human side' *(Psychology, Religion and Healing,* Hodder and Stoughton 1951, p.242). It was a way of co-operating with God at a spiritual level, just as doctors and nurses were forwarding God's healing purposes at a physical level.

It must be recognized, however, that there are difficulties about the concept of intercessory prayer. Why does God appear to respond to some earnest petitions for healing while ignoring others? Is God continuously affecting the workings of nature, changing certain outcomes for the benefit of believers? Or are there spiritual laws in operation which we have as yet failed to understand? Theologians grapple with these problems, but believers are content to live by faith and to rely upon the relationship they have entered into with a loving Heavenly Father. There is ample evidence that our prayers for others *are* often effective.

2

The Sea of Reeds

Preliminaries: Exodus 14 v.15-31 and 'Arm of the Lord, awake, awake!' (H&Ps 433).

Derek: Last month, when we were talking about prayers of intercession, we touched on another question: How does God act in the world? Many Christians believe in a God who *intervenes*. The world goes its own way for most of the time, working according to natural laws, and then God decides to act. He produces an event which may be called a miracle.

That is a crude way of putting it, but it's how many believers do think. They see no problem in this. God is all-powerful, so surely he can do what he likes in his own world. Let's take the story in Exodus 14 as an example. In the Hollywood version of this, in Cecil B. De Mille's biblical epic *The Ten Commandments*, there were great walls of swirling water on either side of the Israelites as they crossed the dry sea-bed. The question is: Did it really happen like this?

Norman: I don't see why not. One of the verses we read mentioned walls of water. It's in the Bible, so that's how it must have happened. As you said, we can't set limits to God's power.

Gillian: I suppose some of the details of the story could be later embroidery. I mean, a certain amount of exaggeration may have crept in as the story was told from one generation to another.

Harry: Even allowing for that, it's a pretty tall story. Things like that simply don't happen. They contradict all the laws of science. Nothing like that ever happens today.

Derek: That's a good point! A young girl, hearing the story for the first time, is supposed to have remarked: 'Mummy, God must have been much more exciting then!'

Norman: Perhaps people had more faith in biblical times. Jesus didn't perform miracles unless he found faith.

Hilda: I'm not sure that's the whole answer. I've sometimes wondered why God didn't do more for all the millions of Jews who died in the concentration camps during the Second World War. God rescued their ancestors from Egypt, but he left the modern Jews to suffer.

Frank: Harry said things like that - like the crossing of the Red Sea, I mean - never happen today. What about the miracle of Dunkirk, when the Channel stayed calm while our troops were being brought back? That was a turning-point in the War.

Hilda: I can remember those days. It was just as remarkable how Hitler ordered his armies to halt when they were about to overrun our forces altogether. What made him do that?

Harry: I don't know much about the War, but didn't this happen sometime during the summer? The good weather could just have been a lucky coincidence. It wasn't an *obvious* miracle like the crossing of the Red Sea.

Susan: Couldn't that crossing too have been the result of good luck? It wasn't the Red Sea the Israelites crossed, but a shallow stretch of water somewhere north of the Gulf of Suez where the Suez Canal now runs. And one verse in Exodus 14 mentions a strong east wind which drove the water back. Perhaps they were able to ford this 'Sea of Reeds' on foot, but when the heavy Egyptian chariots tried to follow they got stuck.

Norman: That's taking all the miracle out of the story. Why try to explain it away? This was a great act of God.

Derek: Perhaps it's time we got a few facts straight. I'm sure Susan has got a point. According to the Bible Commentary I've got, the Hebrew text does say *yam suph* which means 'Sea of Reeds'. Also, the story as we now have it is a blend of different traditions. The verse which mentions the east wind comes from the earliest tradition, what scholars call 'J'. The bit about the walls of water comes from 'P', a much later strand. So there's little doubt the story did develop over the centuries. That's only to be expected.

Norman: It was still a mighty act of God to save his people. I think we're wrong to explain it away.

Gillian: I can see what Susan's getting at, though. What would we have actually seen if we had been there? I saw *The Ten Commandments*, and wondered whether it really happened like that. It was so spectacular, with all the Egyptian soldiers drowning as the waters swept back.

Susan: There's a Jewish story about that. The angels were rejoicing in heaven at the Israelite victory, when they noticed that God himself was downcast. 'How can you rejoice,' he asked, 'when my children are drowning?'

Marion: If God was upset at the death of the Egyptians, does this mean he didn't help the Israelites at all? Are you saying that the whole story is a cooked-up version of a lucky escape? I thought, in my simple way, that the Exodus proves God does save his people. Am I wrong?

Derek: That's an important point, Marion. This tradition is the cornerstone of the Old Testament witness to a Saviour God. But we still have to answer the question: What did God actually *do* at this particular moment in history?

Susan: God certainly inspired Moses to be a great leader. The Israelites wouldn't have escaped at all if Moses hadn't gone back into Egypt and organized the trek to freedom.

Frank: Couldn't we also say that God worked through the east wind, just as he did through the weather at the time of Dunkirk? This would be God working *through* nature, rather than setting the laws of nature on one side.

Derek: That's an interesting point of view, Frank. I've seen miracles defined as events in which faith recognises the activity of God. If you accept that, miracles become a matter of interpretation. When a non-believer would see only a lucky coincidence or a piece of good fortune, a man of faith sees God at work.

Susan: On this view, you would still be assuming that God interfered in some way with the workings of nature. There wouldn't have been a strong east wind, or a period of calm weather during the evacuation from Dunkirk, if God hadn't been pulling the strings behind the scenes. Is that the kind of world we're living in, where God *manipulates* nature when it suits his purposes?

Gillian: But what's the alternative, Susan? You said that God inspired Moses. Do you want to say that God influences human beings, but never affects what happens in the world in any other way?

Susan: Yes, I believe I would want to say something like that. What would happen to the work of scientists, or to historical studies come to that, if they had to allow for a God who was constantly interfering? The regularity of nature, the laws of cause and effect, are basic to such work. Otherwise we'd be back in a pre-scientific world where every event is thought to be divinely caused.

Marion: We're not saying God is always interfering. But the Bible shows clearly enough that God has acted directly at certain times. In fact, the whole Bible witnesses to the saving acts of God. What about the birth of Jesus? What about the resurrection, and Pentecost? Then there's plenty of evidence for miracles, both in the Bible and in our own times. If these aren't acts of God, what are they?

Norman: I feel like Marion about this. What would become of our faith if God *only* works through people? It would involve a drastic revision of the Bible, for one thing.

Susan: I think we must allow for the fact the Bible was written in pre-scientific times, when it was taken for granted many events *were* divinely caused. We find the same attitude today in less sophisticated peoples. It's more natural for us, with our scientific world-view, to interpret events in a different way.

Derek: Our time's nearly up. We must obviously agree to differ on this issue. I recently came across three different definitions of what a miracle is. It's interesting that we've mentioned all three in the course of our discussion. First, a miracle is a violation of the laws of nature. Second, it's an act of God *through* the laws of nature. Third, it's any event which is seen to have a religious significance. So how *did* God act when the Israelites escaped from Egypt? Was it through a spectacular event which violated the laws of nature? Or did God work through nature by means of a strong wind? Or was it perhaps a matter of inspiration - first of Moses, and later of storytellers who were led to see religious significance in the escape?

I don't think we're going to get any further with this question today. Perhaps next month we could consider the Christmas stories, where God is certainly pictured as intervening in history in a dramatic way. Meanwhile, thank you for making this such an easy discussion to lead.

Comment

The escape of the British Expeditionary Force from northern France in late May and early June 1940 was made possible by Hitler's personal intervention. He halted his tanks just as they were about to sweep into Dunkirk. The evacuation was favoured by extremely good weather, although talk of a 'miracle' was probably designed to boost morale at a particularly bleak moment in the War.

It is very difficult to propose a model of God's interaction with the world which is not open to objection. Many people today have a deterministic view of the natural world, and any talk of divine activity suggests to them the idea of someone interfering with the mechanism of a clockwork system. However, the picture emerging from contemporary science is rather of a physical world which is 'in a state of constant and unpredictable flux.' In view of this, one could envisage nature as an open system which includes the possibility of direct divine causation within a framework of regularity and order. The alternative is for the believer to restrict divine saving activity to the sphere of mankind's inner life. God calls and directs, and those who respond act as his agents. This model would involve a self-limitation on God's part, a granting of full autonomy to his natural creation.

3

The Christmas Stories

Preliminaries: Matthew 1 v.18-25 and the carol 'From east to west, from shore to shore' (H&Ps 99).

Derek: You have heard of John Robinson, who as Bishop of Woolwich wrote *Honest to God* back in 1963. Well, four years later he wrote a Fontana paperback called *But that I Can't Believe*. This is how his chapter on Christmas begins: 'But you can't really believe that lot, can you? Stars stopping over cribs, angelic choirs lighting up the skies, God coming to earth as a man - like a visitor from outer space? You couldn't really believe it today. I mean, could you honestly?'

I suggest we should ask ourselves the same question. When we read the Christmas stories from the Gospels, do we believe them literally? Do we expect other people to believe them? When we include them in a carol service, are we putting a stumbling-block in the way of occasional church-goers? Some people in this scientific age must find it difficult to imagine these things actually happening - angels in the sky, a marvellous star guiding travellers to Bethlehem, and so on. What do you think?

Marion: I see no problem. Of course these things happened. This *is* the good news of Christmas, recorded for our benefit by the writers of the Gospels. Christians have always believed these stories.

Hilda: I must say I feel the same way as Marion. What would Christmas be without these stories? I'm not sure I see the point of what the Bishop is saying.

Harry: Well, I agree with this Bishop. For years now I've had my doubts about these events. They're a bit improbable, aren't they? It all sounds like a fairy story, alright for kids but not for grown ups. The whole of Christmas has a sort of unreal atmosphere. Choirs of angels, a magic star ... These things don't happen in the real world.

Frank: I suppose we're so used to hearing these stories, we never stop to think how odd they must sound to some people. But what's the alternative? The stories are in the Gospels. Don't we just have to accept them?

Derek: I'd like to act as Devil's Advocate this evening, since Susan's not here, and argue for a different approach to these well-known narratives. I won't convince you all, but at least you'll be aware there *is* another way of interpreting these passages.

Frank: It would be useful to know what the experts make of them. We do sometimes meet sceptics like Harry here, and we need to know how to answer them.

Harry: Don't get me wrong. I believe Jesus was born in Bethlehem, and I believe he was the promised Saviour. I'm not an unbeliever! It's just that I think the Bishop's got a point.

Derek: The experts don't all agree, of course. The more conservative scholars regard the narratives as historical. But others do regard them differently. The stories *could* be a form of meditation on the scriptural promises. Both Matthew and Luke obviously drew heavily on the Old Testament to explain the significance of Jesus' birth. Take the first chapter in Luke's Gospel. There are close parallels here with the stories about Hannah at the beginning of 1 Samuel. Mary's song - the Magnificat - is very similar to Hannah's prayer in 1 Samuel 2.

Gillian: What are you suggesting, Derek? That Luke made these stories up? I've always assumed Luke got his information from Mary herself when he was in Palestine collecting material for his Gospel.

Derek: That's pure supposition, although much of the information could only have come from Mary if the narratives *are* historical. But most scholars now date Luke's Gospel late in the first century, in the mid seventies or even the mid eighties. That's a long time after the birth of Jesus.

Hilda: You haven't answered Gillian's question. Are you really saying the first two chapters of Luke's Gospel are inspired fiction? I would find that very hard to accept.

Derek: It's possible that Luke had little idea what the actual circumstances of Jesus' birth had been. He's even got the name of the governor wrong. It couldn't have been Quirinius. What I'm suggesting is that Luke tried to express the deeper meaning of Jesus' birth by means of imaginative stories based on Old Testament passages. John also wrote a prologue to his account of the ministry; in his case it was a poem about the Word or Logos becoming flesh. Luke's nativity stories serve a similar purpose.

Harry: That makes sense to me! It's always bothered me how Luke could possibly know what the angel said to Mary, and so on. I'm happy to believe Luke was using his imagination.

Marion: Well, I'm not. I'll continue to believe everything happened just as it's recorded. I don't understand how you can suggest Luke invented these accounts.

Derek: I don't think we should judge an ancient author by modern standards. In those days history was written to *edify* readers rather than to establish the facts. Luke's primary aim was to strengthen the faith of his readers in who Jesus was. He chose a perfectly legitimate way of doing that - through memorable stories based on Old Testament models.

Gillian: I take it, Derek, you're not questioning the teaching of these stories? Surely all that's said about Jesus is true - what Gabriel tells Mary, what the angels tell the shepherds, and so on. If I understand you, it's *that* teaching Luke really wanted to get across.

Derek: Of course. All we're arguing about is the method Luke chose to use.

Frank: What about the accounts in Matthew's Gospel about the wise men and the escape into Egypt? Do some scholars take the same line with those?

Derek: They do, yes. We must remember how eagerly the early Christians searched the Jewish Scriptures for verses they could apply to Jesus. Matthew seems to have built his stories around 'proof texts' of this sort. His main concern was to show that Jesus fulfilled the Scriptures, that he was the Deliverer foretold through the prophets.

Marion: What's wrong with that? We all believe Jesus *was* the promised Messiah, don't we?

Derek: There's nothing wrong with this line of argument in principle, but some of the texts Matthew uses are doubtful choices. Take the famous verse about a virgin who would give birth to a child called Immanuel. When you study that verse in its context in Isaiah 7, you find that the prophet was talking about a sign given to King Ahaz about 735 B.C. It didn't refer to a child that would be born several centuries later.

Marion: There's no reason why an Old Testament verse shouldn't be given a new meaning, is there?

Derek: Perhaps not, but sometimes Matthew seems to have taken that process too far. The verse from Hosea he quotes in chapter two - 'Out of Egypt have I called my son' - originally referred to the Exodus. The quotation from Jeremiah a few verses later, about Rachel weeping for her children, probably referred to the departure of Israelites from the Northern Kingdom in 721 B.C.

Hilda: What follows from this, Derek? That the flight into Egypt and the killing of the children are as fictional as Luke's stories? Before long we'll have nothing left to read at Christmas.

Frank: What about the wise men themselves? Weren't they supposed to be astrologers? I read an explanation of the bright star in some magazine. It was a conjunction of two planets - Jupiter and Saturn, I think. Astrologers could have concluded from that that a new king had been born among the Jews.

Derek: I believe an appearance of a bright comet has also been suggested. But the significant fact is this. The narrative in Matthew 2 contains clear allusions to certain passages near the end of Isaiah, in Isaiah 60 in particular. So these stories, like Luke's, *may* have been inspired by the Old Testament. They contain truth about the identity of Jesus in story form, but they may not be historical reports.

Hilda: What bothers me about all this, Derek, is that it seems to undermine our confidence in the Gospels as accurate accounts of Jesus' life. This can be quite disturbing for some churchgoers.

Derek: I can appreciate that. It raises the whole question of what the Gospels *are*. But you could regard the nativity stories as a special case. After all, they concern events thirty or more years before the ministry of Jesus began. Would reliable traditions about those distant events have been preserved? These stories can be seen as prologues to each Gospel. It looks as though Luke's Gospel, for example, originally began with what is now chapter three.

Gillian: You mentioned earlier the use of these stories in carol services. I must admit, the fairy-tale atmosphere of the readings and carols has sometimes bothered me. But I don't see what can be done about it.

Derek: It's a pity of occasional worshippers miss the heart of the matter because they're put off by things that aren't essential. We shouldn't put unnecessary stumbling-blocks in the way of people who have a genuine difficulty with these narratives. John Robinson, in the chapter we quoted earlier, is very positive about the deeper meaning of Christmas. For some of us the familiar stories still convey the mystery and wonder of Jesus' birth; but for others they bring mystification and a sense of unreality. We must allow for different interpretations.

Harry: Well, I for one feel happier about carol services after this discussion. I shall think of these stories as poetry rather than history in future.

Hilda: You've been an effective Devil's Advocate this evening, Derek! You're right to make us think about things we may have been taking too much for granted, even if we don't agree with all your conclusions!

Comment

It is know that Quirinius conducted a census in Palestine in A.D. 6-7. But if Matthew is to be believed, Jesus was born during the reign of Herod the Great who died in 4 B.C. The governor of Syria in 9-6 B.C. was Saturninus.

Some scholars regard Luke's nativity stories as *Haggadah*, a Jewish form of narration which was seen as 'a legitimate field for the godly exercise of creative imagination' (G.B. Caird, *Saint Luke*, Pelican Commentary, p.30). Luke's purpose was to express his own theological beliefs about Jesus before proceeding with an account of the ministry.

A suitable book for anyone wishing to read more about the nativity stories would be H.J. Richards' *The First Christmas* (Fontana Books 1973).

4

THE HUMANITY OF JESUS

Preliminaries: Matthew 5 v.1-12 and 'Blest are the pure in heart' (H&Ps 724).

Derek: Martin Luther called Jesus 'the Proper Man'. Jesus was man as he was meant to be, in his fullness and perfection. So it's important for us to ask what Jesus was like as a human being. If we are to think of him as our model and ideal, we clearly need to know what he was really like.

First of all, Jesus was a first-century Jew from Galilee. This gave him some characteristics we couldn't share. Jesus thought like a Jew, in concrete images rather than in abstract ideas. So his teaching wasn't systematic and logical - like a Greek philosopher's might be. Jesus also felt like a Jew. He obviously had a deep love for his own people and their traditions.

But what personal characteristics did Jesus have which made him unique, the Proper Man? Let's start with the children's hymn which speaks of 'gentle Jesus, meek and mild'. What do you think of that? Some stores in the Gospels suggest Jesus could be very angry on occasions.

Hilda: Well, Jesus was certainly gentle. That was one of the most wonderful things about him. I'm not sure what being meek and mild means.

Harry: He seems to have been blazing with anger in the Temple. Didn't he set about the traders with a whip?

Derek: That's true. John says he made a whip of cords to drive out the money-changers and traders. He was also angry in a synagogue when some Pharisees tried to trap him into healing on the sabbath [(1)].

Susan: Some scholars doubt whether John's account of the Temple incident is historical. However, Jesus certainly used passionate language in Matthew 23.

Marion: But Jesus had every reason to be angry on those occasions. He wasn't angry on his own account; it was because the Jews were so wrong-headed and sinful.

Gillian: Don't we call that 'righteous indignation'? I've always thought of Jesus as a passionate sort of man who couldn't suffer fools gladly. I remember seeing a film back in the sixties which showed Jesus addressing the crowds like an Old Testament prophet - full of fire and passion.

Derek: You're thinking of Pasolini's *The Gospel According to Saint Matthew*. I took a school party to see that. I agree, there was nothing meek and mild about that Jesus. Does this mean that anger should be part of a Christian's character? It's not listed among the fruit of the Spirit!

Susan: Surely there are things that *ought* to make a Christian angry. We need to define what we mean by meek and mild. Doesn't mild mean the same as gentle? As for meekness, I've seen that defined as 'controlled strength'. Jesus may have been intense and passionate, as Gillian says, but he had his anger well under control. Martin Luther King had that quality; so has Archbishop Tutu. It's made their protests very effective.

Derek: Let's take up these words 'intense and passionate'. Do you think Jesus had a sense of humour? I once knew a minister who was convinced Jesus was without humour altogether. The minister himself was a solemn sort of chap, so he may have been projecting his own outlook upon Jesus.

Hilda: We're told Jesus was a popular guest. He must have been good company. I can't imagine he was always solemn.

Frank: Some of the sayings in the Gospels are quite humorous, aren't they? Like the one where the Pharisees are pictured straining out a gnat and swallowing a camel.

Gillian: Or when a man said he couldn't come to the feast because he'd just got married. The crowds must have been amused when Jesus added details like that.

Harry: Yet I can't imagine it was much fun travelling about with Jesus. The disciples must have been in awe of him. Can you imagine the disciples larking about when they were on the road?

Linda: Shouldn't we be talking about Jesus' love? What made Jesus different was his love for everybody. People were drawn to him because he seemed to understand them and was able to help them. He radiated love wherever he went.

Susan: But it won't do to get too sentimental about this. There was a toughness in his love. Jesus could be gentle and understanding - agreed - but he also made some hard demands on people. I think Harry's got a point. Jesus had a mission to fulfil, and he was single-minded about that. Nothing else mattered to him.

Linda: I can see that, Susan. But Jesus always had time for people in need. The greatest Christians have always shown the same kind of love. Think of Mother Teresa in Calcutta. She's shown us what Jesus himself must have been like.

Derek: That's an important point, Linda. The characteristics of Jesus have been reflected in some of his greatest disciples. And we mustn't forget his offer of forgiveness to the outcasts and sinners. He demonstrated how God was ready to accept anyone who came to him in the right spirit. Nothing offended the pious Jews more than this.

Norman: Don't you think the best description of Jesus is in the Beatitudes? When Jesus gave that teaching he was really describing himself. He depended completely on God, always put God first, and was prepared to suffer in God's service. Each of the Beatitudes describes a side of his own character.

Harry: Jesus didn't mourn, did he?

Hilda: He mourned for Lazarus, whom we're told he loved. But I read somewhere that verse may refer to those who grieve over the sin in the world. Jesus certainly grieved in that sense.

Frank: While we're going through the Beatitudes, what about the one about peace-makers? How does that apply to Jesus? It seems to me he was always stirring up controversy.

Marion: His whole life was devoted to making peace between God and man. He gave his life so that sinners can be reconciled to God.

Derek: Frank is probably thinking about making peace between man and man. The effect of Jesus' ministry was sometimes just the opposite. He said he had not come to bring peace but a sword, and to set people against one another [(2)].

Susan: On the other hand he did urge the Jews to love their enemies. He also created a new community of faith in which old enmities were forgotten. Think of the way he got Matthew the tax collector and Simon the Zealot to work together. They were at opposite poles politically.

Harry: What I don't understand is how Jesus could be perfect. He put God first in everything, he was kind and loving, a great leader - I accept all that. But how could he be human and perfect at the same time? Isn't there a saying, 'To err is human'? Was Jesus different from us, or what?

Norman: The Bible tells us Jesus was tempted as we are, but he never sinned. He always did what he understood to be God's will. He was never disobedient. That's how he was different.

Susan: I believe Jesus was made in the same way as we are. He had the same impulses. He had to *learn* obedience. I imagine he had a very strong prayer life, and always found the strength to do the right thing.

Derek: So would you agree there was an element of *achievement* in the inner life of Jesus? He couldn't have found obedience easy; the Garden of Gethsemane story shows that. Isn't there a case for thinking that Jesus *grew* in understanding and spiritual stature?

Susan: I would say so, yes. This was the result of opening his life completely to God.

Frank: I'm glad you've said that. We're sometimes given the impression Jesus lived on an altogether different level from the rest of us, with advantages we could never hope to possess.

Derek: One month we ought to consider what we believe about the incarnation. Then we could follow up these points in more detail. We started out today asking what Jesus was like as a person. Have we missed out anything important?

Susan: There's his remarkable freedom from prejudice of any kind - racial, social, sexual. His goodwill included everybody, whoever they were.

Linda: Isn't that another illustration of his love? If we're looking for a description of Jesus in the New Testament, what about 1 Corinthians 13 where Paul describes what love is like? I don't know if Paul had Jesus in mind, but it's a wonderful description of Jesus' own character.

Hilda: I hadn't made that connection before, but I'm sure you're right, Linda.

Derek: So if we combine the Beatitudes with 1 Corinthians 13 we get as near to a portrait of Jesus as we're likely to get. I feel we know Jesus a little better as a result of sharing our thoughts this evening. Thank you all.

(1) John 2 v.15 and Mark 3 v.5

(2) Matthew 10 v.34-35

Comment

There has been a re-assessment of anger in recent years; it is now sometimes regarded as an essential part of being human. Thus Kenneth Slack can write: 'The man who can look on cruelty and not be angry is not preserved in some sinless state of calm; he is defective in proper human emotion' (*The Seven Deadly Sins*, SCM 1985, p.74).

There has been a tendency in every age to project upon Jesus qualities which have been admired in a particular culture. Jesus has been portrayed as an ascetic, as one who renounced the world with all its pleasures and possessions. Then during the Enlightenment Jesus was presented as a teacher of social morality, as one who showed men how to live well *in* the world. The variety of images has been bewildering, even within our own century. There is a tendency to see in Jesus what we want to see. It was Albert Schweitzer who pointed out that Jesus was bound to appear 'a stranger and an enigma' to us. It is this very otherness that enables Jesus to challenge our assumptions and values.

5

JESUS' MESSAGE

Preliminaries: Luke 17 v.20-30 and 'The kingdom of God is justice and joy' (H&Ps 139).

Derek: I'm not going to introduce the discussion this evening. *You* are! Our theme is the message of Jesus. I'd like you all to write a single sentence on your piece of paper. Put down what you think was the main *aim* of Jesus during his public ministry. What was he trying to do? Limit yourself to one sentence if you can. There's no need to add your own name. Then we'll look at your suggestions and see how far we agree...

Thank you... Jesus's message must have been determined by his aim. Let's see... 'Jesus came to offer us eternal life' - an echo of John's Gospel there. 'Jesus came to die for the sins of the world' - but that doesn't help us to understand his teaching. We'll need to consider his death another time. 'Jesus offered God's forgiveness to all sinners' - that's certainly true. 'Jesus proclaimed the fatherhood of God and the brotherhood of man' - that gives us a possible theme for Jesus' teaching. This one's apparently written in Chinese... I think it says, 'Jesus came to reveal God's love and to teach us to love' - I'm sure there's an insight there. Some of these sentences say much the same as those I've already quoted... Here's a different idea: 'Jesus' aim was to make us more aware of God and to show us a better way of life.'

Not one of you has used the phrase that was so often on Jesus' lips - 'the kingdom of God' - even though it was the theme both of our reading from Luke and Bryn Rees' hymn. Why not, I wonder?

Gillian: The simple answer is that we're not sure what it means. In any case, you asked us about Jesus' aim, not about his teaching.

Derek: But aren't the two closely related? Some say Jesus' aim was to announce the coming of the kingdom of God, and to prepare the Jewish people for a new age.

Hilda: Are you playing Devil's Advocate again, Derek, and trying to upset our cherished ideas?

Derek: Not today, Hilda. Most New Testament scholars now agree that the kingdom of God *was* the main theme of Jesus' teaching. Near the beginning of Mark's Gospel we read how Jesus came into Galilee proclaiming the kingdom was at hand. He urged people to repent and believe the good news. Most of his parables begin: 'The kingdom of God (or of heaven) is like this...' Then in Mark 9 Jesus says: 'Some who are standing here will not die before they see the kingdom of God come with power.'

Gillian: In that case, a lot seems to depend on what Jesus meant by the phrase. Doesn't it refer to God ruling as king, rather than to a kingdom in the modern sense? I believe we were told that once.

Derek: That's a good working definition. The phrase refers to God actively ruling, exercising his sovereignty. The Jews used the expression - or its equivalent 'the kingdom of heaven' - in at least two contexts. God already rules over those who have accepted 'the yoke of the kingdom', who are obedient to the Law given to Moses. But he will one day impose his rule over all the nations on earth.

Hilda: I've always assumed Jesus was talking about God's rule over individual lives. Wasn't he trying to explain how different life would be if we trusted God more, and obeyed him more faithfully?

Frank: There's a verse which says, 'The kingdom of God is within you.' That supports Hilda's idea.

Derek: That's certainly one way of interpreting the teaching of Jesus - to think of the kingdom as something inward and spiritual. Many Christians still assume that's what Jesus meant. But there's another possibility, which I must admit *does* disturb our set ideas. What if Jesus believed God was about to establish his rule universally?

Norman: Ah! I'm beginning to see where Derek is trying to lead us. The Jews looked forward to the day when God would assert himself, and set up his rule on earth once and for all. He would confound his enemies, right all wrongs, and introduce a new age - the Age to Come. Is this what Jesus was announcing?

Derek: Well, some scholars now think so. It's a possibility we ought to consider.

Harry: Wait a minute, Derek. Let's get this straight. Are you saying Jesus was like a prophet announcing the end of the world? This isn't the picture of Jesus we're usually given.

Derek: Not the end of the world, but certainly the end of the present age. Although there are some passages in the Old Testament which look forward to a time when the earth would be renewed, the deserts made fertile, and so on.

Marion: For once I agree with Harry! This isn't the Jesus we're used to. Why should we interpret his teaching in the Gospels in this way?

Derek: John the Baptist expected a dramatic intervention by God in the near future. There's no doubt about that. Isn't it significant that when Jesus asked his disciples what people were saying about him, many associated him with John? Their preaching must have been similar (1).

Marion: What about the verse Frank mentioned, about the kingdom being within us?

Derek: This may be a mis-interpretation of Luke 17 verse 21. A more accurate translation may be 'in your midst' rather than 'within you'. The whole passage is about the sudden and unexpected arrival of the kingdom. People will be taken by surprise, as they were when disaster struck in the days of Noah and Lot. They will be going about their business when - like a flash of lightning across the sky - the reign of God will be suddenly present.

Gillian: That's all very well, Derek, but isn't there a more serious objection to what you're saying? Things didn't actually happen that way. Aren't you implying Jesus was wrong in what he believed God was about to do?

Derek: Let me ask you a question. What meaning would *you* give to Mark 9 verse 1, about the kingdom coming with power?

Marion: I can answer that. God raised Jesus from the dead, and poured out his Spirit at Pentecost. A new power *was* let loose in the world, the power of the Holy Spirit.

Susan: As one scholar said, if I can quote him correctly: 'Jesus proclaimed the kingdom, and it was the Church that arrived.' But what you're suggesting, Derek, is that Jesus expected something more decisive and final than that.

Hilda: In which case, as Gillian says, we would have to admit that Jesus was mistaken. I don't take kindly to that idea.

Derek: Jesus had a very strong sense of God's presence. We all agree on that. He also thought like a first-century Jew. The incarnation doesn't mean he had a human body but a divine mind. The belief that God would soon intervene in history was widespread at the time. That expectation was in the very air Jews breathed. Jesus must have been influenced by all this.

Susan: I suppose you could argue Jesus was not wrong on essentials. God *was* acting to save his people. Jesus himself *was* God's chosen agent of salvation. Jesus admitted he didn't know everything, such as the time when God would establish his kingdom (2). What Derek's suggesting in no way undermines our faith in Jesus. It just makes Jesus more a man of his time.

Derek: That's right. One of the scholars to interpret the message of Jesus in this way was Albert Schweitzer. He made it clear, in a book called *The Quest of the Historical Jesus*, that Jesus belonged to a different thought-world from ours. We need to make allowances for that. His view of the world, and his religious outlook, were rooted in first-century Judaism.

Linda: We seem to be a long way from the simple gospel about loving God and our neighbour as ourselves. A lot of what's been said this evening has gone over my head. Must we make faith in Jesus so complicated?

Derek: We've been trying to understand what Jesus was actually saying to his contemporaries, what his overall aim was. There *was* a note of urgency in his preaching. That comes out in a number of sayings and parables. It was a time of crisis, a time for decision. Perhaps next month we could consider how Jesus urged people to *behave*. In this way we'll be able to approach the teaching of Jesus from another angle.

Hilda: You've opened up a difficult topic this evening, Derek. At least it should encourage us to look more carefully at what Jesus said about the kingdom of God.

(1) Mark 8 v.27-28 and parallels

(2) Matthew 24 v.36

Comment

Derek has introduced a contentious issue. The teaching of Jesus about the kingdom is many-sided, and it is far from clear how it can be arranged into a coherent pattern.

One recent contribution to the debate has been E.P. Sanders' *Jesus and Judaism* (SCM 1985). In this study Professor Sanders takes as his starting point the well-authenticated sayings of Jesus about the destruction and restoration of the Temple, and argues that this was linked in Jewish though with the *eschaton* or End-time.

One can accept that Jesus as a first-century Jew would have expressed his message in the thought forms of his day, but many Christians - like Hilda - would reject the idea that Jesus could be mistaken about the nearness of the End. What does seem certain, however, is that Jesus anticipated a crisis in the life of Israel as God's chosen people.

6
Sell Your Possessions

Preliminaries: Matthew 6 v.19-34 and 'Jesus calls us! O'er the tumult' (H&Ps 141).

Derek: I want to refer to some ideas in a recent book called *Wolf in the Sheepfold*. The author argues that teaching in the Bible that ought to shock, especially the Sermon on the Mount, has been re-interpreted to make it more acceptable. It has been domesticated to make it conform to middle-class values. Jesus himself, he says, was clearly not a middle-class character. He was somewhat footloose, a charismatic and a miracle-worker, a prophet given to outbursts of anger, and no respecter of property or family. However one describes Jesus, he concludes, 'the word which does *not* come to mind is bourgeois' (1).

This author has a point. Just take the two issues of property and family on which middle-class life is based. Jesus told would-be disciples to sell their possessions. The passage we read from Matthew 6 suggests we should take no thought for the future - no insurance policies, pension schemes, provision for our old age. And what Jesus said about the family gives no support for our modern emphasis on family life. There's some evidence Jesus didn't get on well with his own family (2). He declared that those why obeyed his Father's will were his true kin. Would-be disciples must 'hate' their families for his sake; one was forbidden to 'bury' his father, to stay with him until he died.

I've put the case rather strongly, but there *is* a problem here. How would you respond to it?

Hilda: I've always thought the passage we read from Matthew meant we shouldn't worry, or be anxious about things that don't really matter. It's never occurred to me it had anything to do with insurance policies!

Harry: If Jesus really meant we shouldn't worry about food and clothes, and all the other things we need, he was being unrealistic. He should have tried living on social security for a few months!

Frank: I've often wondered about that. How *did* Jesus and his followers live during the years they were travelling around Palestine? I assume the disciples gave up their jobs and left their families behind. How did they cope without a regular income?

Derek: Well, we read in Luke 8 about certain women who 'provided for them out of their own resources.' The disciples had a common purse for their everyday needs. They must have relied a lot on hospitality. As for their families ... I suppose their circle of relations offered support.

Susan: Going back to what we were talking about last month, perhaps Jesus didn't expect his ministry to last very long. If he believed a new age was about to dawn, there wasn't much point in settling down, acquiring possessions, raising a family. That kind of life would soon be over.

Marion: Surely the point was that Jesus had a mission to fulfil. He couldn't be tied down by possessions and family responsibilities. He had to be free to carry out his mission.

Gillian: Is there any suggestion that *everybody* who accepted Jesus' message should act as the disciples did? I mean, perhaps some of what Jesus said applied only to his full-time helpers, not to people in general.

Derek: That's an interesting point. Perhaps only a few people were expected to sell their possessions and abandon their families. The same has been true all through Christian history. Only a minority of Christians has felt led to live in religious communities, taking vows of poverty, chastity and obedience.

Frank: Doesn't that seem to imply there are two classes of Christians - the élite and the also-rans? I would have thought one group needed the other. Monks and nuns couldn't live the way they do unless they were supported by Christians in the world.

Linda: Aren't monasteries often self-supporting? They don't always depend on other Christians for their living.

Frank: Maybe. But they were given grants of land, and all sorts of bequests, in the first place.

Derek: I don't think we can take that point any further. Does anybody else think parts of Jesus' teaching only applied to a select group of disciples?

Gillian: My point is, Jesus couldn't have been talking to his followers in general all the time. The women Luke mentions obviously didn't leave their homes; nor did friends like Mary and Martha at Bethany. And what would happen today if we *all* abandoned our responsibilities in the world?

Hilda: What teaching of Jesus *does* apply to us, then? I'm beginning to wonder. Gillian says he was making demands on an inner group of disciples. Susan suggests he may have thought the present age would soon come to an end. That seems to let us out altogether. I'd always assumed Jesus was telling *everybody* how God wants us to live.

Derek: It seems to me we're back to last month's question. What *was* Jesus' aim? Let's assume he was trying to prepare the Jewish people for a divine initiative, for a decisive manifestation of God's authority. How would he have done this?

Susan: Wouldn't it be by describing what life in the new age would be like? People needed to wake up to the situation they were in. Time was short. They needed to adjust to God's values.

Derek: Exactly! Thank you, Susan. So Jesus' method, according to some scholars at least, was to undermine the basic assumptions people were making about life. He wanted to disturb their way of thinking, to shock them into a new awareness.

Harry: I'd always thought Jesus used parables to make his teaching easier to understand, as illustrations of the points he wanted to make.

Derek: By and large, Harry, the parables are *not* easy to understand. These stories often have a surprising twist in their tail. Many who heard them would have been puzzled. They would have set people thinking. Some would have seen the point, and would begin to see things differently.

Susan: Like the sound of one hand clapping.

Derek: What do you mean, Susan?

Susan: Well, pupils of Zen Buddhism are told to meditate about something of that sort. It's supposed to be a way of gaining enlightenment.

Derek: I suppose there may be some similarity. Even the parable of the Good Samaritan, which seems straight-forward enough to us, would have shocked - and even offended - some of its original hearers.

Hilda: Would you mind applying this to the passage from the Sermon on the Mount we read earlier? I'm still worrying about my insurance policies!

Derek: Yes. Most of Jesus' audience would have been preoccupied with money worries - taxes and prices, property disputes, and so on. Jesus was suggesting it was time they reconsidered their priorities. 'Set your mind on God's kingdom and his justice before everything else.' There were more important things to consider than the price of fish, and that as a matter or urgency.

Marion: What about other parts of the Sermon on the Mount, about loving our enemies for example? Is that to be explained in the same way?

Derek: Jesus was describing attitudes that would be appropriate in God's kingdom. You could call such teaching 'the ethics of the kingdom.'

Harry: What about turning the other cheek? That doesn't sound very practical to me. I can just imagine what would happen if we took that literally. Everyone would take advantage of us.

Susan: I suppose Derek's argument still applies. Jesus may have been using shock-tactics, trying to jolt people into seeing things in a different way. Turning the other cheek is like the saying about forgiving seventy times seven. It suggests a willingness to forgive on every possible occasion.

Linda: Doesn't the Sermon on the Mount set standards we can never hope to reach? I feel so inadequate when I read that part of the Gospel.

Marion: We have the power of the Holy Spirit to help us. We can't live on a higher level without his inspiration. We must ask for the Spirit's help.

Derek: Can I return to the point made by the author of the book we began with? There *is* a tendency to tone down the demands Jesus made, to interpret his teaching in such a way that it no longer disturbs us very much. We ought to consider whether conventional middle-class values are really compatible with 'the ethics of the kingdom.'

Marion: I do think churchgoers can become too complacent. If we took Jesus at his word, we would have to reconsider a lot of what we take for granted. How *different* is the average churchgoer from everybody else? Most of us conform to this world more than we care to admit.

Derek: It's not for us to criticize other people. We must answer for ourselves. Perhaps in our own Bible reading we should work through the Sermon on the Mount, and decide just how Christians should be different from their neighbours. I'm afraid our time's up this evening.

(1) Robert P. Carroll, *Wolf in the Sheepfold*, SPCK 1991, p.140-141
(2) See Mark 3 v.21, 31-35 and Mark 6 v.4

Comment

The argument for regarding the Sermon on the Mount as 'interim ethics' finds little support today. Some of Paul's rulings, however - as in his discussion of sexual relationships in 1 Corinthians 7 - were clearly based on his conviction that 'the whole frame of this world is passing away'. It is more likely that Jesus was describing the quality of life which would be appropriate within the kingdom of God, life lived in complete dependence upon God. One could argue that such a quality of life should even now be exhibited by Christian communities which anticipate the kingdom and enjoy a foretaste of its blessings. Thus John V. Taylor writes: 'The witness of people who...live as through God's future were already reaching into the present sets up a sign of that future which continues to haunt even those who reject it as unrealistic' (*Kingdom Come*, SCM 1989, p.92).

7

A Minister's Request

Preliminaries: 2 Timothy 3 v.10 - 4 v.5 and 'Powerful in making us wise to salvation' (H&Ps 479).

Derek: I have had a special request from our minister this week. Andrew has asked for feedback on the four sermons he's been preaching on Sunday evenings about Old Testament books. He's now finished the series on 'Historical Fiction'. Before he starts work on another series, he would like to know what people think about them.

Gillian: What has Andrew got in mind for Series Two?

Derek: Well, as you know, he's dealt with Ruth and Jonah, Esther and the first six chapters of Daniel. He's now toying with the idea of four sermons on 'Poetry and Wisdom'. But he obviously doesn't want to carry on if 'Historical Fiction' wasn't well received. It's difficult for him to know what the congregation really thinks. People have thanked him for an interesting sermon after each service, but that may be because it's the polite thing to do! Has the series really been welcomed? There's been no noticeable increase in the evening congregations!

Hilda: I think most people who were there have enjoyed them. I missed the one on Esther, but I got a lot from the others. It's not the sort of thing that's going to attract larger congregations. I don't suppose Andrew expected that. But we all ought to learn more about the Bible.

Harry: What's this about historical fiction? Did Andrew really suggest there's fiction in the Bible? I bet some people didn't agree with that.

Marion: I didn't agree with everything he said. But I can see we can't take everything in the Bible as literally true. I would have liked an opportunity to ask questions afterwards.

Linda: One or two elderly members *were* upset, thought. After the service about Jonah, old Mrs. Simpson said, 'I never thought I'd hear a minister tell us the Bible isn't true.'

Gillian: It's the attitude they were brought up with when they were young. I don't suppose anyone ever questioned the Bible then.

Hilda: I was brought up in the same way, but I've learnt to see things a little differently through the years. There are some parts of the Bible I find very hard to take literally. I'm sure God must intend us to learn something from these stories - even if Jonah *didn't* live for three days inside the stomach of a fish.

Harry: Does anybody still think that actually happened?

Marion: A friend of mine does. She says a sailor did survive being swallowed by a whale about a hundred years ago.

Susan: But that's surely to miss the point of the story. We need to understand the purpose of the book.

Gillian: Andrew said it was a missionary pamphlet. The Jews at the time were like Jonah - reluctant to pass on their religion to other nations.

Frank: And when Jonah finally did what he was told, the foreigners listened to him and repented. I must admit, I didn't know the second part of the story. Andrew's sermon did encourage me to read the whole book through.

Linda: He said something about the book being an allegory, but I didn't follow that very well. Is Jonah supposed to represent the Jewish people, and Assyria the rest of the world?

Derek: That's one way of interpreting the book, yes. The big fish could represent the Exile in Babylon. On the other hand, the book could equally well be a commentary on a verse in Jeremiah, which says that if a nation turns from its evil God won't punish it (1).

Harry: Didn't Jonah ever exist, then? Is he a fictional character like Sinbad the Sailor?

Derek: There is a Jonah mentioned briefly in 2 Kings (2). He was a nationalistic prophet. The author of the book probably just made up a story about him.

Harry: I can see the book's fiction. But why *historical* fiction? What was historical about it?

Derek: The author set his story in an earlier period of history, like a novelist today might write about the days of Queen Elizabeth I. He was probably writing in the fourth century B.C., over three hundred years after Nineveh had been destroyed. Anyway, enough of Jonah... Are there any comments on the series as a whole?

Harry: I'm beginning to wish I'd come to these evening services. What did Andrew say about Daniel in the lions' den, or about those three chaps in the fiery furnace? I suppose that's fiction too?

Linda: I think Andrew shocked a few people that evening. They had always believed these stories were true. I still don't know what to think. God can do marvellous things. He *could* have saved these men.

Susan: It depends on whether you think God protects people from physical danger. Personally, I don't suppose the Jews who first read these stories would imagine they were meant literally. They knew well enough that fire always burns and hungry lions would kill.

Hilda: If I remember aright, that's a point Andrew made. The stories were meant to encourage Jews in time of persecution, when their religion was in danger of being stamped out. The message was that if they stood firm, their people would survive.

Marion: The Bible does seem to need a lot of interpreting. People of Mrs. Simpson's generation used to read their Bibles from cover to cover and believe it all. Nowadays we've got to argue and debate, accept this and question that... Do we end up with a stronger faith or not?

Susan: It does matter how we interpret the Bible. People who believe God will protect them from danger might lose their faith if events prove them wrong. I'm all in favour of learning as much about the aims of biblical writers as we can. When we know their intentions, we're in a better position to understand how their books are relevant to us.

Gillian: I for one would like Andrew to continue with a second series. Are you going to report back to him, Derek?

Derek: That's what he asked me to do, yes. There's a lot of work involved in preparing sermons like this.

Frank: It would help if he could announce the subjects in advance, so that we can take a look at each book before the service. There's only so much of it can be read during the worship itself.

Gillian: What do you think 'Poetry and Wisdom' is likely to include? Have you any idea?

Derek: The two books of poetry would probably be the Song of Songs and Lamentations, and the wisdom books Ecclesiastes and Job. There's an interesting mix for you! These aren't books I would think of preaching about. The Song of Songs is love poetry pure and simple, and Ecclesiastes reads like the work of a disillusioned old man.

Gillian: I've never even read Lamentations. So you can tell Andrew that we're looking forward to Series Two!

Derek: I'll pass on the message. Are there any more comments?

Marion: I hope Andrew isn't going to be too negative in what he says.

God inspired these books for a purpose. We want to know what we *can* believe, not what we can't.

Hilda: He hasn't been negative in the sermons he's given so far. We were left with a positive idea about each book. We didn't come away thinking we needn't bother with those particular books again. He gave us a new interest in these parts of the Bible.

Derek: Good. That's one thing settled. Anything that encourages people to read their Bibles must be welcomed. Now for the bad news... In return for this extra work Andrew is putting in on your behalf, he's asked for a favour. He wants this group to prepare a sermon. Don't be alarmed! It could be broken up into short sections, and no-one is going to be asked to do anything they're not entirely happy about. But if we pool our resources we should be able to work something out.

Gillian: Has Andrew suggested any theme for us to work on? I suppose we ought to take up the challenge. Some of us are used to reading lessons and leading prayers. I'm sure we could put something together. Let's try at any rate.

Derek: The theme Andrew has suggested is: 'How God speaks to us today'. Of course, we could do something different if we liked. But this sounds a promising idea to me. At any rate, think about it, and we'll get down to work next session.

(1) Jeremiah 18 v.8, quoted in Jonah 3 v.10

(2) See 2 Kings 14 v.25

Comment

It is interesting to compare the conclusion of the book of Jonah with that of Nahum, which exalts over the destruction of Nineveh in 612 B.C. Both books end with a question. Nahum implies there is no hope for the Assyrians, no escape from the punishment they deserve. Jonah points out that God pities even this notorious empire. Is the author of Jonah deliberately taking Nahum to task for his narrow nationalism?

It is generally agreed that the book of Daniel was written about 165 B.C. when Antiochus of Syria - nicknamed Epiphanes because he believed he was a manifestation of God - was attempting to crush all opposition to his religious claims. He plundered the Temple at Jerusalem, confiscated copies of the Jewish scriptures, and had them publicly destroyed. Even keeping the Mosaic Law was forbidden. The author of Daniel set his stories in an earlier epoch, when his heroes kept the faith under a different tyranny.

8
A Joint Venture

Preliminaries: 1 Samuel 3 v.1-10 and 'Lord, speak to me, that I may speak' (H&Ps 553).

Derek: The plan this evening is to prepare a sermon on the theme, 'How God speaks to us today.' If we're satisfied with the result, Andrew is prepared to let us take over one of the evening services next month. Since Susan and I are accustomed to leading worship, it might be better if we didn't play too active a part in this. This will be an opportunity for some of you to make your own contribution to an act of worship.

Susan: Can I make a suggestion? Why don't we think in terms of three short talks rather than one twenty minute sermon? Perhaps we could deal with three different aspects of the subject.

Harry: I like it when preachers do that. I find it hard to concentrate on a long sermon, especially when there's a lot in it you need to think about. Breaking it down into bits makes it easier to take in.

Derek: Are we agreed on Susan's suggestion, then - three short talks on different ways in which God speaks to us? Good. Any ideas about how we should start?

Marion: We all know that God speaks to us through the Bible. The Bible is God's word. That should come first.

Gillian: Is it quite as simple as that? I'm not conscious of God talking to me every time I hear the Bible read in church. Sometimes the reading makes little impression on me. I may feel it's not relevant to my situation. It doesn't strike a chord, or meet my need.

Linda: I agree with Gillian. We've got to be in the right mood. Once in a while a reading really hits me. I think, 'This is meant for me.' It's the answer to something I've been worrying about, or it's telling me to do something I've been unwilling to face. I know God has been speaking to me then.

Frank: Occasionally a particular verse comes into your head when you're not in church. I remember once I'd been unwilling to help someone, and I was suddenly reminded of a verse in one of the parables: 'Inasmuch as ye did it not unto one of the least of these my brethren, ye did it not unto me.' That made me feel really ashamed for a time.

Derek: We've probably got enough material here for the first talk. It's just a question of putting it together.

Harry: The first thing we've got to do is get the congregation interested. It's no use just going on about the Bible. We've got to grab their attention.

Derek: What do you suggest then, Harry?

Harry: There's a lot of stories in the Bible where God speaks directly to somebody - to Abraham, Moses, or whoever. Why don't we start with one of these stories, and they say: 'Does God speak like this today? Has he ever spoken to you?' That might make people sit up.

Hilda: We could use the story about Samuel we heard this evening. Then some of us could describe how God has spoken to us. Linda might like to explain one of her experiences, and perhaps Frank could repeat what he's told us.

Derek: Thank you, Hilda. Personal testimony would certainly make a strong impression. Could anyone else contribute in this way?

Marion: Most of you know I was converted at a Billy Graham rally. I went forward because I knew God was calling me. I suppose you could say God spoke through the words of Dr. Graham. So it's not only the words of the Bible God uses.

Hilda: I'm sure God can speak through the words of a hymn or a prayer too. I've felt that occasionally.

Frank: Isn't there also a voice inside our own head? I've no doubt psychologists would say it's only another part of myself. But it could be a way of God talking to us.

Susan: There's a passage in Jeremiah - in fact, more than one - where the prophet seems to be carrying on a conversation with God. At one point he complains God has let him down like a stream that has dried up. Then God answers him. It sounds like a real dialogue going on in Jeremiah's mind [(1)].

Gillian: Christians have often believed God has told them to act in a particular way. I read once that David Wilkerson heard God telling him to leave his country church to work among the teenage gangs in New York. He's the minister who later converted Nicky Cruz.

Derek: I'm sure we could find other instances of that kind of thing in Christian life-stories.

Norman: What about Jackie Pullinger? She felt God wanted her to get on a ship going to the Far East, and when they got to Hong Kong she knew that's where God wanted her to get off. We all know how God used her in the Walled City.

Susan: I sometimes wonder if it was that sort of inner compulsion Abraham felt when he left Ur to seek a new home. The idea that God had long conversations with him may have been a later way of telling the story. I don't believe the experiences of Old Testament characters can have been very different from our own.

Linda: I think another way God speaks to us is by showing us something that needs to be done. I've never heard any inner voices. But sometimes I've been aware of an opportunity, and I've felt, '*I* could do something about that.'

Derek: Thank you, Linda. I'm sure God speaks to us in various ways. We do sometimes become aware of a job that needs to be done, and we are prompted to volunteer. Could anyone else testify to an experience like this? What about you, Harry? How did you come to be a helper in the youth club?

Harry: It was just something I wanted to do. I wasn't aware of God telling me to do it.

Hilda: There was a time when nobody wanted to be church treasurer, and I felt God was urging me to volunteer. It wasn't a job I thought I would be any good at, but we managed without any disasters.

Derek: Perhaps it's time we had a recap. Have we now got enough material for three short talks? We need a brief introduction...perhaps Harry could do that. Then the first talk, about how God speaks through the Bible...could that be shared by Marion and Linda?

Linda: I couldn't speak for long, but I expect I could give one or two examples from my own life.

Derek: Good. What about you, Marion?

Marion: If you amended that to God speaking through the Bible and preaching, I could say something about my conversion experience. I could explain how God spoke through Billy Graham.

Derek: That's fine. Now the second talk, about how God speaks through an inner voice...your experience would be relevant, Frank. What about a husband and wife team? Perhaps Gillian could say something about David Wilkerson.

Gillian: If I can find the details. Or I suppose I could find another example in a book of biography.

Derek: Good. That leaves the third talk, about God opening our eyes to opportunities for service. I wonder if you could help us out, Esther - with Hilda?

Esther: I could mention the time I offered to help with the crèche, if you like. But, like Linda, I wouldn't want to speak for long.

Hilda: I'm sure we could work something out, if we set our minds to it.

Derek: Alright. Now the readings before each talk should be easy enough to choose. This evening's reading about Samuel before the first talk... The passage about Jeremiah - if you can find the reference for us, Susan - before the second... As for the third, what about the story in Acts about how Ananias was told to find Saul after his vision on the road?

Gillian: Is that really about becoming aware of an opportunity, Derek? I'm not sure that fits our third theme very well.

Frank: What about that story in Isaiah where he says, 'Here am I. Send me.' That might fit better. There was a job to be done, and God wanted to know who would go for him.

Hilda: We don't all get a vision before we're asked to take something on! It can all happen in a very ordinary way. We don't want to give the wrong impression.

Norman: If I may just make a suggestion... Do you remember Paul's dream about a man of Macedonia who implored Paul to help his people? There's a clear case of Paul becoming aware of a need, and responding to it [(2)].

Derek: Thank you, Norman. That sounds like a more appropriate story. We're still left with the choice of hymns and prayers. Perhaps two or three of us could consult about that nearer the time.

Hilda: This makes us realize how much is involved in preparing a service. I wouldn't like to do this every week.

Derek: Well, we can tell Andrew we're ready to go ahead. Thank you all for your help.

[(1)] Jeremiah 15 v.15-21

[(2)] Acts 16 v.9

Comment

In biblical stories the dream is often a medium of communication with the divine. One thinks of the Joseph saga in Genesis, or the nativity stories in Matthew's Gospel. The dream Paul had at Troas is particularly interesting. Paul had felt impelled to hurry through Asia Minor on his 'second missionary journey'. Did the vision of a Macedonian prompt a complete change of plan, or was the thought of taking the gospel into Europe already forming in the back of Paul's mind? In any case, Christians are frequently aware of God going before them, opening up new and unexpected avenues of service.

9

THE EMBARRASSMENT OF THE OLD TESTAMENT

Preliminaries: 1 Kings 22 v.10-28 and 'Deep in the shadows of the past' (H&Ps 447).

Derek: I want to start with a piece of church history this morning. Let me tell you something about Marcion, who taught some unorthodox views between about 144 and 160 A.D. According to him Christianity is a Gospel of Love, and because of this he rejected the Old Testament altogether. He believed the God revealed in the Old Testament was a *different* God from the one proclaimed by Jesus. The Jewish God created the world and issued the Law, but apart from that he was capricious, despotic, and cruel. He would eventually be overthrown by the God of Love whom Jesus came to reveal.

The communities Marcion founded didn't last very long. But his views illustrate a problem I think we ought to face squarely. The Old Testament *can* be an embarrassment to Christians. I can still remember how, many years ago, a colleague on the staff drew my attention to a particularly gruesome passage in 1 Samuel. The prophet Samuel apparently hacked a captured king to pieces 'before the altar of the Lord' (1). 'There,' my colleague said. 'What do you think of that? And you call this book the word of God!'

Well, what *do* we think of that, and of all the other bloodthirsty bits in the Old Testament? How *can* such stories be 'the word of God'?

Susan: I'm sure Marcion had a point. God is certainly credited with some odd behaviour in the Old Testament. Take the story when Abraham was told to sacrifice his only son Isaac. I shall protest the next time anyone suggests God was testing Abraham's faith. What sort of God would test obedience in this way? Abraham must have suffered agonies during that journey to the mountain. It would have been heartless and cruel to inflict such suffering deliberately.

Marion: I don't have any problem with that story. God does test our faith, and Isaac came to no harm in the end.

Harry: I bet he would never want to go for a walk with his dad again! I agree with Susan. The story doesn't put God in a very good light.

Derek: What did you make of the story we read from 1 Kings? Hilda?

Hilda: I'm not sure I understood the reference to a lying spirit. Could you explain that?

Derek: According to this story, God deceived Ahab by promising him victory. What God really wanted to do was to entice Ahab onto the battlefield, where he would be killed.

Linda: Stories like that aren't read in church. In any case, people in those days didn't have a very clear idea about God. How could they? This was hundreds of years before Jesus showed what God is really like.

Derek: The problem lies in our use of the Old Testament. When any part of the Bible is read in church, we usually say, 'This is the word of the Lord' or some such phrase. We assume the Bible has a special status. Yet it contains some very strange material.

Hilda: But, as Linda says, the doubtful passages are never read in church. The preacher, or those who make up the lectionary, only choose passages that are helpful to us.

Derek: I accept that, Hilda. But on what grounds do we pick and choose? Are some bits 'the word of God' and not others? And what do we mean by 'the word of God' anyway? We no longer believe God dictated every word of the Bible to men who simply acted as his secretaries.

Susan: That's just what Muslims do believe about the Qur'an. God dictated every word to Muhammad. So the Arabic text is quite literally the word of God.

Marion: I've got a friend who believes much the same about the Bible. It's no use arguing with her. Everything in the Bible, so Anne says, is exactly what God intended it to be.

Frank: Didn't Billy Graham keep on saying, 'The Bible says this...The Bible says that'? He must believe the Bible word for word.

Marion: Not like Anne does. I find it hard to explain, but you do have to test everything in the Bible in the light of Christ. He is the Truth.

Harry: So you accept that some writers in the Old Testament got things wrong? They had wrong ideas about what God was like, about what he wanted?

Marion: I'm not sure about that. But they didn't understand God as well as we do today. I do find some stories difficult to explain - like this one about the lying spirit.

Gillian: What about all the laws in the Old Testament that don't apply any more? All those regulations about animal sacrifices, for example. We don't stone adulterers any more.We could cross through several pages in the Old Testament with a blue pencil and be none the poorer for it.

Susan: I've met the occasional Christian who would be happy to do without the Old Testament altogether. Some parts of it are an embarrassment when we're trying to commend the Father of Jesus Christ.

Derek: But there's another side of this, of course. Jesus himself was nurtured on the Hebrew Scriptures. They were his inspiration. We should never forget that. More than once he claimed to be fulfilling the words of Isaiah [(2)]. He freely adapted Old Testament imagery in his own teaching. He seems to have endorsed the Law of Moses, even through he did go beyond it in some of his demands.

Frank: I think Gillian ought to go easy with her blue pencil. The Ten Commandments are still basic, aren't they? So is the teaching of the prophets about social justice. There's a lot that carries over into Christianity.

Norman: And what about the Psalms? There's nothing like those in the New Testament. I can't understand how Christians can manage without the Old Testament altogether.

Harry: Alright! So parts of the Old Testament are still valuable. But there are plenty of dodgy passages too. What about the command God is supposed to have given to slaughter all the inhabitants of captured cities? How bloodthirsty can you get? If God really *didn't* give these orders - to Joshua or whoever - why do we still say it's all 'the word of God'?

Derek: That's the key question, Harry, and we haven't got much nearer to answering it yet. Susan?

Susan: I hope I wont offend any of you by saying this. You can put me right if you like! I see the books of the Old Testament as *human* products. I'd say the same about the New Testament, but let's stick to the Old Testament for the moment. These books were written by men who often had a limited understanding of God. They were influenced by the ideas of their time, by the culture they lived in, and so on. Sometimes they showed remarkable insight, but at other times their vision was limited. We must interpret all they wrote in the light of the glory of God as revealed in Jesus Christ. I agree with Marion there.

Norman: It says somewhere in the New Testament that all Scripture is inspired by God [(3)]. Susan has said nothing about inspiration. Does she mean that some parts of the Old Testament are more inspired than others?

Susan: That's a difficult one! Perhaps I could ask you a question in return. What do you mean by inspiration? Is the Song of Songs, for example, inspired in a different way from the sonnets of Shakespeare? Was the author of Chronicles more inspired than John Bunyan when he wrote *Pilgrim's Progress*? I find the idea of inspiration very difficult in relation to some parts of the Bible. Then there's this glib phrase 'the word of God'. What exactly do we mean by that? I believe Christians have a lot of hard thinking to do on these issues.

Hilda: I do believe God speaks to us through the words of the Bible. We agreed on that last month when we were preparing our service. I've heard someone say that God uses human words to convey *his* word.

Derek: That's a neat way of putting it. It's been suggested that when the Bible is read in church we should say, '*Listen for* the word of the Lord.' In other words, if we are attentive God can speak to our hearts and minds through the reading.

Linda: In that case, why wouldn't any other book do equally well? Why use the Bible, if God can use any human words to speak to us?

Derek: The Bible does speak of God's dealings with his people. I suppose it's the subject matter which makes it the appropriate medium for God to use. After all, the Bible does contain the foundation documents of our faith. Every book within it bears witness in some way to what God has done.

Susan: God can speak through poetry and legend as well as prophecy and law. That's the point the hymn we sang this evening was making.

Derek: Good, Well, our time's up. We've been dealing with important issues, and I'm sure we'll have to face them again in future sessions. We'll leave it there for the moment.

(1) 1 Samuel 15 v.32-33.

(2) See Luke 4 v.16-21 and Luke 7 v.21-22

(3) 2 Timothy 3 v.16

Comment

The status and authority of the Bible is an issue which divides Christians across denominational boundaries. One comment made by the great Swiss theologian Karl Barth expresses a point of agreement. He said that the Bible is the word of God 'not by reason of the book itself but by reason of the use which God's Spirit can make of it when we read it.'

One recent book which could be warmly recommended as a general introduction to the Bible is John Barton's *What is the Bible?* (SPCK 1991). When dealing with the passages in the Old Testament commanding the destruction of the native Canaanite inhabitants of Palestine (for example, Deuteronomy 7 v.1-2), Barton comments: 'They are a warning against any theory of biblical authority in which all parts of Scripture are to be held in equal honour and regarded as equally binding' (op. cit., p.105).

10
Gospel Truth

Preliminaries: Mark 1 v.1-13 and 'When Jesus came to Jordan' (H&Ps 132).

Derek: I've decided to deal with a well-known New Testament story this evening - the baptism of Jesus. We've been concerned with questions like the meaning of inspiration and the authority of the Bible. Last month Susan remarked that the books of the Bible are human products whose writers display different levels of insight. Let's see how such an approach could affect our reading of the Gospels.

We'll take Mark's account of the baptism first; it's usually reckoned to be the earliest. Let's imagine Mark with pen in hand and a blank sheet of papyrus before him, ready to begin his Gospel. What is he setting out to do?

Marion: Wasn't it to provide information about Jesus, about what he said and did?

Gillian: I assume he wanted to strengthen the faith of his readers, to encourage belief in Jesus as their Saviour and Lord.

Derek: That's a good start! So in his opening section he obviously wanted to make it quite clear who Jesus was. He needed to show that Jesus fulfilled the hopes of the Jewish people. So he quotes a passage from Isaiah and tells us a little about John the Baptist's message. Now he wants to introduce Jesus himself... How is he to do this?

Hilda: There must have been stories circulating in the church about how Jesus was baptized by John. Mark may have heard one of the original disciples tell the story.

Derek: But how would anybody have known what had happened to Jesus on that occasion? What would an eye-witness have been able to report? Was the voice from heaven like a public announcement?

Hilda: Put like that, I suppose it sounds unlikely. I've always imagined the voice being inside Jesus' head.

Susan: Some commentaries say the words are a double quotation from the Old Testament - from Psalm 2 and Isaiah 42, if I remember rightly. Perhaps these particular passages came vividly into Jesus' mind as he stepped out of the water.

Gillian: I believe I see what Derek's getting at. How would anybody else know this? I suppose Jesus might have described his experience to the disciples months afterwards.

Marion: Surely God would have told Mark what to write. God could have put these words into Mark's mind.

Derek: Does inspiration work that way? Isn't it more likely that Mark himself put this quotation together in order to make clear to his readers who Jesus was? He wanted to show that Jesus was the Messiah of David's line, and also perhaps the Servant spoken of by the Second Isaiah.

Frank: Just a minute, Derek. Are you saying there was no divine voice, that the whole story was made up by Mark himself?

Derek: I've no doubt Jesus *was* baptized in the Jordan, and that this was a decisive experience for him. But I can't see how anybody would know what went on in his mind.

Susan: What you're saying is, this whole passage is written for the benefit of the reader. It tells the reader who Jesus is, and sets the scene for the story of the ministry.

Derek: Exactly. This introduction serves the same purpose as the nativity stories in Matthew and Luke, or the famous prologue about the Word in John.

Linda: Can I ask about the dove that came down from the sky? Surely everyone would have seen the Spirit coming to Jesus in this way?

Derek: Well, what do you all think?

Hilda: It said in my Bible notes that the Spirit entered Jesus *like* a dove - in other words, in a peaceful and gentle way. Apparently when God's Spirit came to people in Old Testament times, they sometimes behaved in unusual ways.

Norman: That's right. Samson killed a thousand Philistines with the jawbone of an ass; Saul danced about and prophesied (1).

Gillian: Doesn't one of the Gospel writers actually say the Spirit was in bodily form, or have I got that wrong?

Derek: No, your memory is not playing tricks. Let's turn to Luke's account of the baptism. It's in chapter 3 verses 21 and 22... There's the very phrase - 'in bodily form'. It's been suggested this has a symbolic meaning. Luke meant that Jesus was endowed with the Spirit in a complete and permanent way. Other men of God had only received the Spirit on a temporary basis, as it were.

Gillian: I notice Jesus was praying at the time.

Derek: Yes. Most of the turning points in Luke's Gospel take place in the setting of prayer. Now let's look at Matthew's version of the same incident. You'll find it in chapter 3 verses 13 to 17...

Frank: I see John didn't want to baptize Jesus. Why was that? Did he already know who Jesus really was? I thought Jesus was a relation of his, a cousin.

Susan: This looks like an addition Matthew made to the story he found in Mark. Isn't it supposed to meet a difficulty some Christians had with the original account? John baptized 'for the remission of sins' but Jesus was believed to be sinless. So why did he need to be baptized in the first place? This extra paragraph in Matthew supplies a reason.

Hilda: The older translations used to say, 'For thus it becometh us to fulfil all righteousness.' That phrase has stuck in my mind. I often used to wonder what it meant. Here I see it's put much more simply - 'We must do all that God requires.'

Marion: Is Susan suggesting that Matthew made this bit up? If we go on like this, there won't be anything left in the Gospels we can still believe actually happened.

Derek: We're not going to agree on issues like this. We must agree to differ! There's no doubt the Gospel material took shape to meet the needs of the early Christians. We must try to understand their problems and preoccupations. If belief in Jesus' sinlessness led to arguments about the baptism story...well, yes, I can imagine some teacher suggesting John must have felt unworthy to baptize Jesus. Don't you think the story could have developed in this way?

Susan: To be fair, some scholars lay more stress on the creative role of the church than others do. I suppose this conversation between Jesus and John may actually have taken place, but it's odd that no other Gospel mentions it.

Linda: I can sympathize with Marion, though. The approach you're suggesting leaves us very uncertain what happened and what didn't. I'm sure when most Christians read the Gospels they assume it's all true.

Derek: That raises the question of what you mean by 'true'. However, let's complete our study of the baptism stories. You'll find John's account in Chapter 1 verses 29 to 34. I'll give you a moment to read it through...

Harry: This seems to be quite different from the other accounts. According to this, the coming of the Spirit as a dove was a sign given for John's benefit. How do you square that with what Hilda said earlier on?

Derek: The question is whether we should *try* to square it with the other accounts. Perhaps we should accept the four different versions on their own terms, and learn what we can from each.

Linda: But why should John's account be so different?

Derek: It's usually said that John wanted to affirm the superiority of Jesus over the Baptist. In Asia Minor where the Fourth Gospel was probably written there were groups who still looked to the Baptist for their inspiration rather than to Jesus. There's evidence for that in Acts. So in this Gospel the Baptist is shown bearing witness to Jesus as the Son of God and the Lamb of God. The contrast is also made between water baptism and baptism with the Spirit [(2)].

Frank: I'm beginning to realize we ought to find out more about the intentions of the Gospel writers. I can see how this has affected the way they have presented their material.

Marion: But I still believe most of what they tell us is reliable.

Derek: Before we finish, perhaps we ought to turn briefly to the questions that were troubling us last month. In what sense are these four accounts of the baptism 'inspired'? What authority do they have as 'the word of God'? What do you think, Gillian?

Gillian: The writers were obviously guided by God to write what the early churches needed, to strengthen their faith in Jesus. What else can we say?

Marion: Only that the Gospels still have that power today. People are still converted when they read these stories of Jesus' life. They are led to accept Jesus as their Saviour and Lord.

Norman: What John says at the end of chapter 20 applies equally to all four Gospels: 'These things were written that you may believe Jesus is the Christ, the Son of God; and that through believing you may have life in his name.'

Derek: That's the right point with which to end this evening. Perhaps we should understand the authority of the Bible as a whole in a similar way. It brings men to God, and God to men. It produces faith, and changes lives.

[(1)] Judges 15 v.14-15 and 1 Samuel 10 v.5-6

[(2)] Acts 19 v.1-7

Comment

Since the early years of the church attempts have been made to 'harmonize' the Gospels; one such work, the *Diatessaron* of Tatian, was used in Syriac-speaking churches for centuries. But it has now become clear that the four Gospels tell differing stories, in spite of the literary relationship between Matthew, Mark, and Luke. Any modern reader who tries to 'harmonize' the nativity or the resurrection narratives soon realizes how incompatible the different accounts are. Any attempt to reconstruct the life of Jesus is fraught with difficulties.

This does not mean, as some radical scholars have suggested, that we can know practically nothing of the historical Jesus. But it *does* mean that we see Jesus through the post-resurrection faith and the theological presuppositions of each evangelist. This has the effect, as John Barton suggests, of directing our attention 'away from exact biography and towards an engagement with the whole shape of his character and purpose' (op. cit., p.90).

11

An Interview with Paul

Preliminaries: 2 Corinthians 4 v.5-15 and 'O what shall I do my Saviour to praise' (H&Ps 569).

Derek: After the undoubted success of your service about how God speaks to us, I would now like to present you with another challenge! I am due to conduct an evening service at Notbury Methodist Church next month, and I would welcome your help. The idea is to interview Paul, to imagine he is being questioned about his career while in prison in Rome. I only need two people to take an active part in the service, but I thought we could all discuss the interview this morning. We could decide what questions we would like to ask Paul if we had the chance, and what his answers might be. In other words, I need help to prepare an outline script. I could rehearse the two volunteers nearer the time. What do you think?

Frank: It's going to be a little difficult deciding on Paul's answers, isn't it? If we knew what Paul would say, we wouldn't ask the questions in the first place!

Derek: Ah, but as a group - and with a little research - I think we could work out Paul's views. The average congregation probably knows very little about Paul - apart from the fact he was converted on the road to Damascus, went about on missionary journeys, and wrote a few purple passages like 1 Corinthians 13.

Gillian: It sounds a good idea. It would make a change from the usual kind of sermon. Perhaps you could divide the interview into two parts, so that people won't have to concentrate for too long at a time. Would it all be written down?

Derek: No. It wouldn't sound very spontaneous if we were just reading a script. But we would need to decide the questions and answers in advance. I believe interviews on radio and television are often rehearsed beforehand. It's not all done off the cuff.

So, there's the challenge! Perhaps we could first discuss Paul in general terms, and then see what the most promising questions are likely to be. Who would like to start?

Linda: We could ask Paul why he persecuted the Christians before his conversion on the way to Damascus. I've never understood why he hated them so much.

Harry: People might find that a bit boring. It's all so long in the past. I'd rather tackle him on some of his controversial views. Why was he so much against women, for example? The congregation would sit up and take notice if you got Paul to explain his opinions on that subject.

Marion: What makes you think Paul was so opposed to women, Harry? I haven't got that impression of him.

Harry: Well, he wasn't married for a start. Or did he have a wife who's never mentioned? Then he tells one church no one should marry unless they really had to. And didn't he tell women they must always obey their husbands? He's hardly the patron saint of Women's Lib.

Derek: Harry's got a point. The congregation would be interested in why Paul held views like that. There's also at least one passage where he urges women to keep silent in church!

Susan: To be fair to Paul, there *is* another side to this question. At the end of some of his letters - Romans 16 is a good example - he greeted some women as his co-workers. He accepted they had an important role in the pastoral and evangelical work of the church. He also says in Galatians that in Christ there is no more male and female; the barrier of sex is broken down [(1)].

Derek: Let's look at one or two of the passages Harry referred to, and see what we can make of them. Have you all got a New Testament handy? Good... Now where's the chapter in which Paul gives advice about marriage?

Susan: I think you'll find it's 1 Corinthians 7... The bit Harry was thinking of is in verses 8 and 9. But you'll find the explanation for this further on in the chapter. Look at verses 26 and 29: 'In a time like this it's best for a man to stay as he is... The time we are living in will not last much longer.' Paul believed the end of the age was near, so there was no point in undertaking new responsibilities.

Frank: What exactly did he believe was going to happen, Susan?

Susan: There's a description of the end-time in 1 Thessalonians. There will be a trumpet call, Christ will descend from heaven, and all of his followers will be united with him.

Harry: And then what? Will they all be taken off to heaven?

Susan: It seems more likely Paul thought Christ would reign on earth. A verse in Romans 8 suggests the earth will be transformed, and nature 'set free from bondage and decay'.

Harry: So according to Paul there's no point in getting married, because life as we know it isn't going to last much longer.

Susan: That's about it. It may also explain why Paul wasn't a social reformer. I mean, he says little about slavery. There was no point in trying to change society if the end was so near.

Gillian: But in that verse from Galatians you mentioned it also says something about slaves and free men, doesn't it? That barrier was broken down too.

Susan: Indeed. When Paul sent the runaway slave Onesimus back to his master, he urged Philemon to treat him as a brother. Yet nothing was said about giving Onesimus his freedom.

Derek: We seem to be making some progress. I take it Paul's priority was to convert as many people as possible before the end came. Then those who had faith in Christ would be saved, and those who didn't would perish.

Susan: When Paul wrote to the church at Rome he was planning a missionary journey to the west, to Spain in particular. He said he had completed his work in the eastern half of the Roman world (2). He may have believed God had called him to convert a representative number of Gentiles before the end.

Hilda: He must have believed time was short, if what you say is true. I've always admired his energy, his constant travelling. And I suppose he wrote a lot more letters than we now have in the New Testament?

Susan: There are references to letters which haven't survived (3). The burden of pastoral care must have weighed heavily upon him.

Frank: I get the impression, from what I've read of Paul's letters, that he wasn't an easy man to get on with. He's often telling people off, or attacking those who disagree with him. All those arguments about the Law and circumcision... Was there something important at stake?

Derek: The big issue, as I understand it, was how people qualified for salvation. Some of his opponents - who were Jewish Christians like himself - wanted all Gentile converts to become Jews. You could only join the community of believers in that way.

Harry: That's all very well, but what's it got to do with being a Christian today? A congregation would soon switch off if you went into these arguments about the Law of Moses. Who cares about that now?

Gillian: I must say Harry's got a point. Galatians isn't my favourite New Testament letter, and I always get bogged down in Romans when Paul develops his views about the Law.

Norman: I should have thought the basic question, 'What must I do to be saved?' is still important.

Frank: Well, Derek. How would Paul have answered that question?

Derek: Trust in God's saving action in Christ, and experience new birth in the Spirit. That's the short answer. Paul insisted that faith in Christ was the only qualification. This opened salvation to Jew and Gentile on equal terms. If Paul hadn't won this argument, the history of the church would have been quite different.

Hilda: Paul had been brought up a Pharisee, hadn't he? It must have been difficult for him to set all this on one side.

Derek: He certainly had a lot of rethinking to do after his Damascus experience. He agonized a lot over the Law. But he couldn't get away from the fact that God had now acted *in Christ* for the world's salvation.

Harry: You keep talking about salvation, and being saved. That's another thing I'm not clear about. Saved from what, exactly?

Derek: In a word, sin. Paul seems to have thought of sin as a cosmic force which held men and women in its grip. Being baptized and entering the Christian community freed people from sin's power. It was like a slave receiving his freedom, or a condemned man being acquitted. It gave a wonderful sense of release.

Frank: There's another thing about Paul... I'm not sure how to put this, but I sometimes feel he's remote from us. His experience, his way of thinking, are different from ours. Where's the point of contact?

Hilda: My Bible notes have been dealing with 1 Corinthians recently. There's plenty of contact there - party spirit, spiritual pride, not making everybody feel equal in the church... Human nature hasn't changed much, even among Christians!

Susan: We haven't said anything about the transformation of human nature. According to Paul, anyone who is 'in Christ' becomes a new person. There's a new creation [(4)]. There's surely plenty in this teaching to challenge us today.

Hilda: I think we've just about exhausted our ideas about Paul. Has this discussion been of any help, Derek?

Derek: Oh yes. I think I'd better represent Paul myself in the interview. Then I would only need one or two helpers to ask the right questions!

Hilda: I don't expect the congregation will want anything too complicated. If you reawaken their interest in Paul's letters, and send them home determined to read one or two of them for themselves, you'll have achieved your purpose. We wish you well.

(1) Galatians 3 v.28

(2) Romans 15 v.18-19

(3) 1 Corinthians 5 v.9 and Colossians 4 v.16

(4) 2 Corinthians 5 v.17

Comment

There is little doubt that some of the ways the women members of the congregation were behaving at Corinth offended Paul's sense of what was seemly. This might account for the 'hard sayings' about the role of women to be found in 1 Corinthians 11 v.2-16 and 14 v.34-35. These seem to be out of harmony with Galatians 3 v.28 and Paul's practice of including women among his fellow-workers. There is another 'hard saying' in 1 Timothy 2 v.11-15, where women are told to listen 'with due submission' and not to exercise any authority over men.

Some scholars deny that Paul wrote the 'hard sayings' at all. The Pastoral Letters are regarded as post-Pauline; 1 Corinthians 14 v.34-35 is said to be a later insertion into the text of the letter. But 1 Corinthians 11 v.2-16 is not so readily explained away.

The crucial question is whether Paul was expressing permanently valid principles, according to which men and women are meant to have different roles in the church, or merely giving instructions for a particular cultural situation. In the latter case they need no longer be regarded as normative in our different cultural setting.

12
MISUSING THE BIBLE

Preliminaries: John 8 v.31-47 and 'In Adam we have all been one' (H&Ps 420).

Derek: I want to give you two examples of how the Bible has been misused. Do you know the story in Genesis 9 where Noah curses his son Ham for seeing him naked as he lay in his tent? 'You will be a slave to your brothers', he says. Well, until recently that curse was used by the Dutch Reformed Church in South Africa to justify apartheid. Since Ham was regarded as the founding father of the Negro race, it was asserted that black people were destined to serve the whites. The curse of Ham was still effective!

Now consider what we read this morning from John 8. The Jews were charged with being children of the Devil. For many centuries in Christian Art Jews were depicted worshipping the Devil as their natural father. There has been a terrible record of anti-semitism in Christian Europe. From time to time Jews have been massacred. This has been justified by appeal to verses in the New Testament, particularly the words in Matthew's Gospel where the Jewish crowd says to Pilate: 'His blood be on us, and on our children!' (1)

It seems to me we have a problem here. The Bible is often used to back up attitudes and beliefs we would condemn. In this way the Bible is abused. Perhaps we could think of a few more examples, and then consider what principles are involved.

Susan: I once met a British Israelite in a church I was visiting. He gave me some literature which made out the British people are descendants of the ten lost tribes of Israel. There was a string of quotations from the Bible to prove the point. I'd never read such nonsense.

Hilda: I've not heard of the British Israelites. Are there many of them?

Susan: I looked them up in a reference book when I got home. Apparently there are about two million of them. They believe that Britain - which includes the Commonwealth countries and the U.S.A. - has inherited the promises made to Israel in the Old Testament. Not only that, but our Queen is a direct descendant of King David. I don't know if her Majesty is aware of that fact!

Gillian: I don't know about British Israelites, but I have tried arguing with Jehovah's Witnesses. They certainly know their Bible. I found it hard to answer them point by point. I kept saying, 'Well, *our* church doesn't believe that.'

Derek: The interpretation of the Bible is an important issue here, as with all these unorthodox sects. They are using different principles, and coming up with different meanings. On what basis do we decide who is right?

Susan: Surely it's often a question of evidence. To go back to the British Israelites, there's just no convincing evidence of a link between the tribes who were deported in 721 B.C. and the English-speaking peoples today. It's all baseless conjecture.

Frank: I was going to ask about Ham. I believe Noah had three sons. How did Ham become connected with the black races in South Africa? *Is* there any connection?

Derek: None at all! It's just a tradition that grew up over the centuries, without any basis in fact. Has anyone else thought of an example of how the Bible has been misused?

Linda: Aren't women supposed to be weaker than men because it was Eve who caused Adam to sin? Some say that proves women are inferior or more sinful.

Marion: That reminds me of something I read about a Scottish surgeon in the last century. He refused to use anaesthetics in childbirth because Genesis says, 'In sorrow thou shalt bring forth children.' The pain was meant to be part of Eve's punishment (2). All women must suffer because of Eve's fault.

Frank: To go back to Derek's other example, about the Jews. That bit about the Jews having the Devil for father... Did Jesus really say that, or didn't he?

Derek: Many Christians, I'm sure, assume that John's Gospel reports the actual words of Jesus. For my part, I believe we're hearing John's voice rather than that of Jesus in passages like that. What do you think, Susan?

Susan: I'm inclined to agree. Some scholars call John's Gospel 'a creative re-working of the tradition'. In other words, it's John's distinctive interpretation of Jesus. Some have said there's an anti-Jewish bias in this Gospel. It was probably written when there was a lot of ill feeling between Christian groups and the Jewish synagogues.

Frank: What about that verse in Matthew's Gospel - 'His blood be on our heads'? I assume the Jewish crowd did say that?

Derek: There seems to be a general tendency in the Gospels to blame the Jews for the death of Jesus. The villains in the Passion story are Caiaphas and the chief priests. Pilate, especially in Matthew's Gospel, is let off the hook.

Norman: Isn't that a fact of history? The Jews *were* mainly responsible for having Jesus killed.

Derek: The final decision did lie with Pilate. In any case, it makes no sense to blame all subsequent generations of Jews for what happened at Jerusalem so long ago. There's no justice in that. Guilt can't be inherited, whatever Christians in earlier centuries may have thought. We don't blame Germans living today for the atrocities committed under Hitler.

Norman: But the Jews still don't accept Jesus as the Messiah, do they? They still refuse to acknowledge him.

Derek: That's no excuse for persecuting them. Some Jews do study the New Testament, you know. They accept Jesus as a rabbi and a holy man. But they don't look at these traditions through the spectacles of Christian faith.

Gillian: Where is all this leading us, Derek? We've seen how some people use the Bible to support their own mistaken ideas, or to justify their own prejudices. Others approach the Bible without our kind of faith. It's almost as though everybody finds in the Bible what they want to find.

Derek: It's true we all read the Bible with certain beliefs already fixed in our minds. We can't escape from that situation. All I'm suggesting is that we should be aware of the fact, and take account of it as far as we can.

Susan: A lot of trouble is caused because people impose a meaning on the text it was never meant to carry. Gillian mentioned the Jehovah's Witnesses. There's one verse in Revelation about the redeemed in heaven - one hundred and forty-four thousand of them. One Witness assured me those people would all be from their organization [(3)].

Derek: He would, wouldn't he! But I'm sure you're right. We must always begin with what the text originally meant. That's where we need all the scholarly help we can get. Then, of course, the passage is sometimes reinterpreted within the Bible itself.

Norman: How do you mean, Derek? Are you talking about how Old Testament verses are fulfilled in the New?

Gillian: I thought you argued, when we were talking about the Christmas stories months ago, that some of the connections made with Jesus were rather artificial? I can remember you saying something about the quotations found in Matthew's birth stories, for instance.

Derek: That's true. But in general terms the early Christians were surely right to see Old Testament hopes fulfilled in Jesus. Take the story in Acts where Philip is talking to the Ethiopian in his chariot. The Ethiopian was reading Isaiah 53, you remember, and he asked, 'Who was the prophet talking about?' Philip was fully justified in witnessing to Jesus.

Marion: When Andrew dealt with the Song of Songs, he said that both Jews and Christians interpreted the book in a religious way. First of all it was just love poetry. Then the Jews said it described the love of God for Israel. Later on Christians thought it spoke of the love of Christ for the Church.

Derek: Several parts of the Bible were interpreted allegorically in earlier times. Passages which seemed to be about one thing were said to be really about another. The trouble is, by that method you can make a passage of Scripture mean practically anything you like! That's why I think, like Susan, that the original meaning of the text is so important.

Hilda: I'm beginning to appreciate the problem you mentioned at the beginning. What *does* have the authority to interpret the Bible in the right way? Do we leave this to the scholars, or to church leaders, or do we trust our own common sense? Even if we say the Holy Spirit will guide us, he seems to guide different people to different conclusions.

Derek: There's the dilemma! Scholars don't agree among themselves, and no Protestant is going to submit to the kind of direction over faith and morals the Roman Catholic Church claims over its members. That leaves our own conscience and common sense.

Susan: Perhaps we're wrong to suppose there *is* only one correct way to interpret the Bible. We must allow for diversity among Christians, and also for the possibility of new truth breaking forth from the words of Scripture. It took eighteen centuries for most of Christendom to realize slavery was contrary to God's will. We haven't yet worked out the implications of Paul's statement, 'In Christ there is neither male nor female.' Perhaps one day there'll be a black woman Pope at Rome!

Derek: With fierce arguments for and against such a development, all based squarely on the Bible! It is difficult to see how we can ever escape from that situation. Perhaps we had better get on with our prayers of intercession!

(1) Matthew 27 v.25

(2) Genesis 3 v.16

(3) Revelation 14 v.3

Comment

The Bible has provided an inexhaustible quarry for proof texts to support any number of bizarre theories. Nothing illustrates more clearly the importance of critical-historical study to determine what the texts meant in their original setting. This ensures at least some control over the process of interpretation.

In recent years the importance of historical criticism has been under attack. Some have argued that the meaning of a text is to a significant degree determined by the response of the reader; there is no point in seeking a single authoritative meaning for any literary text. But there are considerable dangers in that approach. The *primary* meaning of any passage of the Bible is the one the author intended to convey to the audience he was addressing. If that meaning is not regarded as normative, there is no check on any reader's prejudices or flights of imagination.

After this particular meeting of the Thursday Group most of its members were in no hurry to leave. Two or three expressed an interest in undertaking a systematic study of the Bible. Susan recommended two books by Etienne Charpentier, a French priest who understands the needs of adult education groups. They are called *How to Read the Old Testament* and *How to Read the New Testament* (both published by SCM). For lighter reading, Derek recommended *The Good Book* by Brian Redhead and Frances Gumley (Duckworth 1987).

The question also arose of what topics should be discussed during the following year. It was decided to work through the Apostles' Creed in order to consider the basic tenets of the Christian faith. It was realized this would be a daunting task, but a necessary one if they were to be prepared to explain their convictions to others.

Part Two
The Apostles' Creed

13
Believing in God

Preliminaries: Isaiah 40 v.12-25 and 'God is a name my soul adores' (H&Ps 24).

Derek: The Apostles' Creed begins: 'I believe in God, the Father almighty, creator of heaven and earth.' I'm going to suggest we concentrate on the second phrase - 'the Father almighty' - this evening. Since childhood we've probably all thought of God as our heavenly Father. But the use of this image has been under attack. Some, for example, accuse us of wishful thinking. Like children, we feel the need for Someone to turn to when things get rough, when we are unable to cope: so we project the image of a loving Father into the sky.

Others argue that Fatherhood is an unhelpful image for those people who've had an unhappy relationship with their natural father. For many children today the most significant adult is their mother, or perhaps even a grandparent. Then there are the feminists who insist God isn't exclusively masculine. God is our Mother too. Should we, perhaps, think of God as our heavenly Parent?

These are just three reactions to the traditional image of divine Fatherhood. So we need to be clear what we understand by it, and why we continue to use it. What point would you like to consider first?

George: I'm glad you've brought this question out into the open. No offence intended to others present, but I've always thought the idea of a loving Father in the sky a bit childish. I believe in God, of course, but he's a universal Spirit - not a kindly old gentleman helping me out when I'm in trouble.

Hilda: I don't believe he's a kindly old gentleman either, George. Please give us credit for growing up a little! But God *is* in some ways like an ideal Father, in his love for us and in the way he treats us.

Susan: But George does have a point. Childish ideas have great staying power. How many grown-up Christians still *do* think of God in such a way? I guess a good many! There's also the question of how far these biblical images can be taken. As Hilda says, God may be in some ways *like* a father, but he is not literally our Father - any more than he's literally a stern Judge or a powerful King. If you push these images too far, they soon begin to contradict one another.

Marion: I like the idea that God is our Mother too. This reminds us of different aspects of God's love for us. Why *should* God always be referred to as 'he' and 'him'?

Gillian: The trouble is to think of an alternative. We can't always be saying 'she' and 'her', and to refer to God as 'it' is definitely a step in the wrong direction. But I'd like to go back to what Susan said a moment ago. How does she suppose different images contradict one another? Aren't they - what's the word I want? - complementary, expressing different aspects of the truth?

Susan: I was thinking of the father in the prodigal son story. He forgave his son for what he had done, whereas a judge would have imposed some punishment. Then think of how a king demands obedience as of right, whereas a loving parent doesn't expect affection on those terms - especially when the child has come of age.

Norman: Are you suggesting that some images are nearer to the truth about God than others? On what grounds can we pick and choose? I agree with Gillian. All the images in the Bible tell us something about God.

Derek: We do have a standard by which to judge. As someone has said, 'God is Jesus everywhere.' God must be entirely Christlike. Any images which give a different impression must be challenged.

Susan: I'm sure you're right. Is God really like a Warrior whose garments are stained with the blood of his enemies, as one Old Testament passage makes out [(1)]? That's surely a projection of human feelings of revenge.

Frank: I've been wondering about this word 'projection'. Would I be right in thinking that *all* our ideas about God are projections? I mean, we can't imagine what God is actually like, so we use pictures taken from the life we know. Isn't this true of everything we say about God?

Derek: That's an important point, Frank. God is beyond our imagining. When we try to contain him within our own thoughts, we're in danger of losing a sense of mystery and awe. We must guard against the tendency to talk as though we knew all there is to know about God.

Marion: But we do have the Bible. Surely we believe God has revealed himself to us through the Bible. This knowledge has been given to us. God wants us to know him better.

Susan: There's a verse somewhere in Second Isaiah which speaks of God hiding himself [(2)]. I've often wondered about that. God hasn't made himself too conspicuous. We believe he's in the background, behind everything that exists - the source of all being. Yet other people can look at the world and conclude that all talk of God is meaningless.

George: That's a point that's often bothered me. Why *doesn't* God make himself more conspicuous? We can hardly blame people who say there's no evidence he really exists.

Marion: I don't know how you can say that. There's the Bible, the teaching of Jesus, the witness of the Church, the evidence of the world around us... That should be enough. If people choose to ignore God's revelation of himself, that's their look-out!

Hilda: I think that's a little harsh, Marion, if you don't mind me saying so. I've talked to people who find it very hard to believe there's a God who cares for us like a father. Their experience of life hasn't made faith easy for them.

Gillian: I've read somewhere that people who knew emotional security and affection when they were children are more likely to believe in a loving God than those who didn't. They find trust easier to give.

George: So belief in God really depends on our upbringing. It's not a matter of free choice. Is that what you're saying?

Derek: Can I try to answer that? Belief in God does involve trust, trusting the universe, believing that in the end our ideals will be vindicated. Trusting that, in spite of appearances, there is 'a power working for righteousness'. People who've had an unhappy childhood, or who've been badly let down by someone they depended on, could find this basic trust difficult.

George: So much of what we believe seems to depend on our experience of life. If things have gone well for us, and we've enjoyed plenty of affection, then God's in his heaven and all's well with the world. But others have found life cruel and the world a friendless place. *They* aren't going to trust in a heavenly Father who looks after them, protects them from harm, and the rest of it.

Marion: I don't think you're right, George. These are just the people who respond so gladly to the good news about Jesus. When they're converted they see the world in a different way. I didn't think much about God until I went to a Billy Graham rally. Now I *know* God is my Father who cares for me personally. I've had that confirmed time and time again.

Derek: Thank you, Marion. George does have a point, though. There's so much tragedy in the world, so much undeserved suffering, that people *do* wonder how far a loving God is in control. Perhaps we should go on to consider this problem next month. After all, the Creed does call God 'almighty'. Could he have arranged things differently? Esther, you look as thought you would like to say something...

Esther: Well, it's only that... Don't we call God our Father because Jesus taught us to? We were told once that Jesus used a word which meant 'Daddy'. He must have felt God was very close to him, to speak to him like that.

Gillian: I was once talking to a friend who had been to Israel for a holiday. One day on a bus she saw a little Jewish boy cuddle up to his father and call him 'Abba'. I believe that's the same word Jesus used.

Susan: There's more to it than that. According to Paul, the Spirit enables *us* to address God in the same way - calling him 'Abba! Father!'(3) That's a wonderful privilege, when you come to think of it. It shows the intimate kind of relationship open to us as Christians.

Derek: That would be an appropriate point with which to end. Are there any other comments you would like to make?

Frank: While we're talking about belief in God, what do you make of the opinion polls which suggest over seventy per cent of people in this country still do believe in God? I find that encouraging. Belief can't be at such a low ebb.

Susan: It all depends on what they understand by the word 'God'. These polls never ask people to elaborate on their beliefs. I suspect many believe in a kind of life-force, or even in the power of fate. How many of that seventy per cent actually believe in the Father of our Lord Jesus Christ?

Derek: Not many believe strongly enough to want to worship him in church! But we do need to try to understand those who find Christian faith difficult. The problem of suffering must be a stumbling-block for some. We really must face this issue in our next session. Thank you for your contributions this evening.

(1) Isaiah 63 v.1-3
(2) Isaiah 45 v.14
(3) Romans 8 v.15

Comment

George asked at one point in the discussion why God does not make himself more conspicuous. Some writers have gone so far as to speak of the deliberate hiddenness of God, a hiddenness which is necessary if men and women are to be completely free in their response to him. As John Hick has written: 'Perhaps he has deliberately created an ambiguous world just in order that we shall *not* be compelled to be conscious of him' (*The Second Christianity*, SCM 1968, p.47). Or as Pascal said: 'There is enough light for those who only desire to see, and enough obscurity for those who have a contrary disposition' (*Pensées*, No. 430).

It is the conviction of Christian believers that God has revealed his presence and his character through the actions to which the Bible writers bear witness,and supremely through the events surrounding the life and proclamation of Jesus Christ.

14

UNDESERVED SUFFERING

Preliminaries: Romans 8 v.18-25, 31-39 and 'God is Love: let heaven adore him' (H&Ps 36).

Derek: We're going to tackle a problem this evening that taxes the brains of the wisest scholars. It's often called the problem of evil. God created all that exists. God is good. Yet there is a great deal of evil in the world - both moral evil in the hearts of men, and undeserved suffering due to disease and natural catastrophes. We might do no more than skirt the fringes of the problem, but if we're going to defend our faith effectively we ought to have some provisional answers ready.

I suggest we try to focus our thoughts on two specific situations. A baby dies of leukaemia, and the mother in her grief demands to know why God allows such a terrible thing to happen. A much-loved son, with a promising career before him, is killed in a car crash caused by a driver the worse for drink. The father asks: 'Why? Why *our* son?' You may already have tried to answer such heart-felt cries for understanding. If not, you may well be challenged to do so in the future. What can you say? Hilda?

Hilda: When Christine Burrows was dying I tried to help Gordon, who was more bewildered than bitter. It's not easy to see why anyone so young should die of cancer. It was a help for Gordon to know God shared in his grief, like the hymn we sang suggested. When human hearts are breaking, there's the same ache in God's heart. I'm sure Gordon was also helped by our prayers, as I've said before.

George: I wouldn't have known what to say to Gordon. What *can* you say, except offer sympathy. I'm surprised he still comes to church, and hasn't lost his faith. I would have felt very bitter if I'd been him.

Susan: I don't think people want a theoretical explanation for suffering in those circumstances. They want to feel the support of their friends - and perhaps of God himself. But that doesn't mean we shouldn't seek some explanation for ourselves.

Hilda: Job, in the Old Testament, suffered terribly and demanded an explanation from God. But he didn't get one! What he did get was a vision of God's power and wisdom. Perhaps that's the only answer we can expect.

Derek: I've seen it suggested that the Cross reveals how God is involved in the sufferings of the world. Like Hilda, I'm impressed by those words in Timothy Rees' hymn.

Marion: I thought Jesus was bearing the sins of the world when he was on the cross. Jesus' death was the result of *moral* evil, surely.

Derek: I take your point, Marion, although I think the cross may indicate more than you're suggesting. Perhaps we can discuss that another time. What about the problem I mentioned at the beginning? God created the world, so he must be in some way responsible for the existence of cancer and leukaemia, and other painful diseases.

Gillian: I hate the thought of God sitting in his celestial office and 'sending' diseases to particular individuals. Some talk of this or that illness being God's will. I can see God must *allow* such things to happen, but that's not the same as saying he actually *wills* them.

Derek: A good point, but why does he even allow them? The fact is that disease and decay seem to be built into nature. This is the way the world is, with malaria-bearing mosquitoes as well as harmless butterflies.

Norman: Hasn't the world gone wrong because of human sin? That's the teaching of the Bible, in the book of Genesis. The world was perfect when God created it; he pronounced everything 'very good'. When Adam and Eve were disobedient all sorts of evils entered into the world, including disease and death.

Susan: I must disagree with you there, Norman. There's no evidence for a sudden change in nature when man appeared. Nature was always 'red in tooth and claw'. The basic workings of nature haven't been affected by falling angels or human sin. You can't shift responsibility from the Creator in that way.

Derek: When God pronounced everything in nature 'very good', it's sometimes taken to mean that the world suited his purposes. God has allowed life on earth to develop in the way it has, because it's in such a world his purposes can come to fruition.

Frank: People who have been struck by tragedy and illness are not going to find that easy to accept! So much suffering seems to be pointless, something that could have been avoided if God has arranged the world in a different way.

Hilda: Aren't we back to the story of Job? Job had to learn that God knew best, even though God's purposes were not explained to him.

George: What's all this talk about God's purposes, anyway? Have we any clue what these might be?

Derek: A Christian would say God's purposes have been revealed in Christ. The goal of creation is the development of Christlike men and women. The end of the process has already been revealed.

George: I don't see how that explains why nature is like it is. What's the connection?

Susan: I'm intrigued by the passage we read from Romans 8 where Paul says all creation is groaning as though in childbirth. The end product, as it were, is the appearance of the children of God. So this world provides an environment capable of producing spiritual beings in communion with God.

George: That sounds like the old-fashioned idea of the earth as a place of soul-making. Are diseases and disasters supposed to help in this process? They may bring out good qualities in some people, but more often they're simply destructive. There's no way they can contribute to human fulfilment.

Hilda: Paul does say, in a verse we left out this evening, that in everything God works for good with those who love him. God *can* redeem the most hopeless situations, and bring good from the worst of circumstances. I do believe that.

Frank: It strikes me there would need to be another life for God to pick up the pieces. I'm thinking of that baby Derek mentioned who died of leukaemia. I once saw an inscription on a child's grave: 'A bud on earth but a bloom in heaven.' So many people fail to reach their potential in this life. If God's trying to produce spiritual children, he needs more time than this life allows.

Derek: That's a powerful argument for life after death. If we have understood God's purposes aright, then this life must be only the first stage in the process. But we're still left with the question: Why is Stage One placed in such a setting as this?

Frank: I can see that moral evil must exist if people are going to be free to decide how to act. Take the young man killed by a drunken driver Derek mentioned earlier. If people are going to be free to behave badly, accidents and tragedies are bound to happen. God could hardly design a world where we are protected against the selfishness of others.

Derek: That certainly accounts for the suffering caused by crime or war. But it doesn't explain natural evil - disease and handicap, drought and earthquake, and so on.

Susan: I was reading somewhere that there's a lot of freedom in the way nature works. Perhaps *randomness* is a better word. A hundred years ago scientists used to believe the world was a complex machine, working mechanically, with everything predictable. Now, it seems, the picture is different. There *is* order, but there's also scope for surprising developments, unpredictable variations. The whole structure is looser than was once thought, more random.

Perhaps we ought to imagine God letting nature go its own way, rather than closely controlling it. That's a difficult idea, and I haven't expressed it very well. But if God lets human beings do their own thing, whatever the consequences, perhaps he has given a certain freedom to the universe itself.

Gillian: Christians usually think of God being completely in control. What you're saying, Susan, seems to contradict this. I imagine God *guiding* evolution, so that man emerged from more primitive forms of life.

Susan: I'm not competent to give you a scientific answer, but I believe there were a number of variations that led nowhere, new developments that proved to be dead ends.

Derek: I'm beginning to see what Susan's getting at. This randomness in the universe may be necessary to forward God's purposes - even though it has led to the emergence of viruses and cancerous cells, and produces natural disasters from time to time.

Hilda: I would find it difficult to explain all this to the parents of a baby who had died of leukaemia! That's the situation we started with. Are we any nearer knowing what to say?

Linda: I haven't followed all of this. But we could assure the parents that the child is still in God's care, and that God's purposes for the child haven't been defeated. There's comfort for grieving parents in the Bible.

George: So if someone hit by tragedy says: 'Why me? Why does God allow it?' do we just reply: 'In this world anything can happen. That's the way God has let the world develop, and we've just got to trust him'?

Hilda: Adding, George, that if we can accept what's happened and co-operate with God, even the darkest tragedy can produce some good.

Derek: We've all had to think hard this evening. We can't see through the mystery, but at least we know we needn't be afraid of it. There's an answer for the heart, if not for the head. It's not an empty platitude to say that underlying everything are the everlasting arms.

Comment

One of the most persuasive attempts to solve the problem of evil is that made by John Hick in his *Evil and the God of Love* (Fount 1979). According to this line of argument, the universe has to be the way it is if God is to achieve his goal of 'person-making', a process which begins in this world and continues in eternity. But the further question of whether this end is *worth* the misery of children, the pain and anguish so many human beings suffer, remains a matter of trust rather than of rational demonstration.

15
WAS JESUS DIVINE?

Preliminaries: Philippians 2 v.1-11 and 'Can we by searching find out God?' (H&Ps 76).

Derek: I know we said we would work through the Apostles' Creed, but I'd like to begin this evening by quoting a few phrases from the Nicene Creed. This was formulated in A.D. 381 at the Council of Constantinople; it is included in the A.S.B. and the Methodist Sunday Service.

The section about Jesus says that he was 'God from God, Light from Light, true God from true God... of one Being with the Father.' It goes on: 'For us men and for our salvation he came down from heaven: by the power of the Holy Spirit he became incarnate from the Virgin Mary, and was made man.'

Now let me quote from a famous hymn by Charles Wesley which speaks of 'Our God contracted to a span, Incomprehensibly made man.' The second verse begins:

> 'He laid his glory by,
> He wrapped him in our clay;
> Unmarked by human eye,
> The latent Godhead lay...' [1]

It is this language about Jesus we have to make sense of. In the traditional story of the incarnation, the Son was in heaven with the Father but came down to earth and assumed human nature. Is this a literal account of eternal realities, or is it a picture-language way of explaining the significance of Jesus, a significance we could now express by a different 'story'?

Gillian: Are we competent to deal with these issues, Derek? We're not trained theologians. I'm afraid we're soon going to be out of our depth on this subject.

Derek: I take your point, Gillian. But it says in 1 Peter we should always be ready to defend the hope that is in us [2]. We *should* be able to explain in our own way what is central to our faith. I've been trying to persuade the Reverend Arthur Wilkins to come along and help us on theological issues. As some of you know, he's a retired Methodist minister living at Notbury. Arthur has agreed to come later in the year.

Marion: I don't see there's anything to discuss. This is what Christians believe - that God sent his Son into the world to save us. We either believe that, or we don't.

Derek: Well, what about the verse we read from Philippians which says Jesus 'emptied himself' when he came to earth? What aspects of his divine nature did he leave behind?

Gillian: When he was in a human body he could only be in one place at one time. He was obviously limited in that way.

Derek: What about his powers?

Linda: He could work miracles. That proved he was divine. No ordinary man could have done what Jesus did.

George: I must take you up on that. I don't want to start an argument about miracles - which you may have had before - but some of the stories in the Gospels seem a bit far-fetched to me. Jesus turning water into wine, stilling a storm, walking on the water... It all reminds me of those films about Superman. He came from another planet as a baby, and had all sorts of superhuman powers. Some Christians seem to think of Jesus like that, as a visitor from outer space. I want to think of Jesus as a *man*, as one of us, not as a divine being in disguise.

Marion: But Jesus *claimed* to be God, George. 'He who has seen me has seen the Father,' he said. 'I and the Father are one... Before Abraham was, I am' (3)

Susan: I take issue with you there, Marion. It's most unlikely those were the actual words of Jesus. There's a lot of John's own theology in the Fourth Gospel. Think of the risen Christ in glory speaking through John if you like. But I can't imagine Jesus making claims like that during his earthly life.

Derek: That's an important point, if you're right! What claims *did* Jesus make for himself? If Jesus was divine he must have been aware of the fact.

Marion: He taught with authority; no one disputes that. 'Moses told you this. . . but I tell you this and that.' And he forgave sins; as the scribes said, only God could do that. And he says somewhere that anyone who receives him receives God. I don't think that's in John's Gospel (4).

Susan: That need only imply that Jesus was acting for God. His authority derived directly from God. That's not the same thing as claiming he *was* God.

Hilda: I would like to know how to answer Derek's question. Who *did* Jesus claim to be? Aren't the experts agreed about this?

Susan: You don't get a clear answer from the scholars. The evidence from the Synoptic Gospels - Matthew, Mark and Luke - suggests that

Jesus didn't welcome the title of Messiah. It had too many political overtones. He seems to have preferred the title Son of Man, but it's far from clear what he meant by it.

Linda: What about the title Son of God? If Jesus was the divine Son of God as the Creeds say, he must have known who he really was.

Norman: Surely there's plenty of evidence Jesus knew he was the Son of God. There's his baptism and the transfiguration, as well as the claim he made somewhere in Matthew that nobody knew the Father except the Son [(5)].

George: That may be so. But my point is this. Jesus was either one of us, or he wasn't. Was he on our side of the line, so to speak, or was he a sort of God-Man with one foot in each camp? That's a crude way of putting it, but you see what I mean. I'll give you an example. The Virgin Birth story bothers me. If you take it literally, it suggests Jesus was *not* a full member of the human race. He only inherited genes from his mother, whereas other characteristics were brought in from outside.

Marion: But this was necessary. He *had* to come in from the outside, as you put it. Human nature was hopelessly corrupt. There had to be a fresh start if the human race was to be redeemed. Jesus was 'made in all points like we are, yet without sin', as the Bible says [(6)].

George: In that case, how can Jesus be our example? If he was essentially different from us from the start, with spiritual advantages denied to us, how can we be expected to follow in his steps?

Derek: I can see what George is getting at. He wants to think of Jesus starting where we are, and pioneering a new way of living in close communion with God - like a mountaineer climbing a mountain peak, and then guiding others along the same route. Is that what you have in mind, George?

George: Something like that, yes. I've talked too much this evening.But I want to get right away from the Sunday School picture of Jesus with a halo round his head, always calm and serene, and performing impossible miracles with a lift of his hand. I don't think he was like that at all.

Derek: Don't apologize, George. We're all glad you have spoken out. Perhaps our idea of Jesus *is* too pious and conventional. What do others think?

Frank: I've sometimes wondered about the temptations of Jesus. Was there ever a real chance of him making a wrong decision? If there was,what would have happened if he had made one? Would he still have been the Messiah?

Susan: That's an interesting point, Frank, and it links up with what George was saying. I've heard the suggestion that Jesus was only *provisionally* God's agent, so long as his will remained in perfect accord with God's.

Marion: I find that idea ridiculous. Jesus *was* God's Son, and always had been. How could he lose his status? He was tempted, but he was always stronger than Satan.

Hilda: I'm finding this discussion rather unsettling, but I'm glad we've brought up these questions. I've come to think of Jesus living by faith as we have to do, not always knowing what the future held for him, and having to trust his Father to show him the way.

Derek: Do you think he ever had doubts, Hilda?

Hilda: I'm not sure. He certainly knew disappointment. And why was he so distressed in the Garden of Gethsemane? Was it fear, or was there some other reason?

Gillian: I've sometimes thought he was uncertain what to do. He had to be sure he was doing the right thing. All this makes Jesus much more *human* than he is often made out to be. I agree with George about Sunday School pictures of Jesus. I remember seeing one in the schoolroom of a village church. I can see now how sentimental and unrealistic it was.

Derek: Our time is nearly up. Where have we got to? Some of us have been anxious to stress the genuine humanity of Jesus. But we haven't got to grips with the question of how this fits in with other claims we want to make about him. I wonder if we could begin next session with that issue. We've taxed our brains hard enough for one evening!

(1) From 'Let earth and heaven combine' (H&Ps 109)
(2) 1 Peter 3 v.15
(3) John 14 v.9, 10 v.30, and 8 v.58
(4) Matthew 10 v.32-33, 40 and parallels
(5) Matthew 11 v.27
(6) A combination of Hebrews 2 v.17 and 4 v.15

Comment

In some popular expositions of Christianity the argument is advanced that since Jesus claimed to be the divine Son of God, he must either be believed or dismissed as mad. This supposed dilemma discounts the possibility that Jesus made no such claims during his lifetime. It may be questioned how far the Fourth Gospel contains the actual words of Jesus, rather than an inspired meditation upon the early tradition. Some scholars have distinguished between 'earthly sayings' delivered by Jesus during his life on earth, and 'heavenly sayings' made by the exalted Christ through his spokesmen in the early church. The verses quoted by Marion in the discussion (see note 3 above) may belong to the second category.

16
AN ALTERNATIVE STORY

Preliminaries: Hebrews 1 v.1-9 and 'Christ, our King before creation' (H&Ps 75).

Derek: Last month, if you remember, we were stressing the humanity of Jesus, the belief that he was in every way 'one of us', one who knew trials and temptations, disappointment and doubt. We didn't get to grips with the problem of how Jesus can be thought of as 'sent from heaven' or 'revealing God to us'. We're all familiar with the traditional story of the incarnation. Last time I hinted there might be an alternative story that would convey the significance of Jesus in a different way. I've had a word with Susan about this, and she's agreed to outline one such story this evening. We thought we would ask Arthur Wilkins to introduce a discussion on the atonement next month.

So, over to you, Susan...

Susan: I'm reminded of the saying about fools rushing in where angels fear to tread! What I'm going to use is an account of a book called *God as Spirit*. This was written back in the 1970's by a Professor of Divinity at Cambridge, Geoffrey Lampe [(1)]. What Professor Lampe does is suggest another way of understanding the relationship between Jesus and God, an alternative story to set alongside the traditional idea of 'God the Son' becoming flesh.

He invites us to think of God in every age trying to transform human beings. He has always been at work 'saving' humanity, and trying to coax a personal response from us. God's purpose has always been to deliver us from selfishness and to make us whole, to bring us to fulfilment as spiritual beings.

Jesus is at the very centre of this process. God and man united in Jesus, and in him the goal of creation, the purpose of evolution, is revealed. In other words, God is at work creating Christlike people.

This is where New Testament talk about the Spirit comes in. The Spirit isn't a sort of impersonal energy. The Spirit *is* God, the outreach of God in person, God's very presence in his creation. Now Jesus always remained completely open to God as Spirit. Sin is resistance to the Spirit, the Spirit of love. But Jesus 'died to sin', as Paul says. There *was* no resistance in Jesus, at any point in his life. God as Spirit and the human spirit of Jesus were perfectly united.

I think I'd better pause there. Perhaps there are questions you'd already like to ask. I can see that Marion is bursting to speak!

Marion: What you say is all very well, Susan, but what's wrong with the traditional story - as you call it? Why do we *need* a new way of 'explaining' Jesus at all? Believing that God sent his Son into the world has brought countless people to salvation. It's the very heart of our faith.

Derek: I think we were skirting round that problem last month, Marion. If you remember, we began with the idea that the divine Son 'emptied himself' when he came to earth. Doesn't that suggest that in some ways the incarnate Son was *less* than his Father in heaven, lacking some of the attributes that belong to God?

Then we had George saying he wanted Jesus to be one of us, sharing our humanity in every way, and not like some visitor from another dimension. It is difficult, on the traditional account, to think of Jesus being *fully* divine and *fully* human at the same time.

Susan: Yes. There's a sentence near the beginning of Professor Lampe's book making that very point. I put a marker in the place in case it was needed. Here it is... The theological model of 'God the Son', he writes, suggests 'either that deity revealed in human terms in Jesus is somehow other than God whom we conceive of as Father, or that God whom we acknowledge in Jesus was united with him with something less than a fully human personality' (2). According to teachers in the early church, Jesus assumed a human nature that was *impersonal*. It is difficult to see what sense we could make of that idea today.

Gillian: I've sometimes wondered what Charles Wesley meant when he said God 'wrapped Him in our clay'. That sounds pretty impersonal!

Marion: What Susan has told us sounds plausible enough, but is it based on Scripture? I mean to say, is it just this Professor's bright idea, or is it supported by the New Testament? The New Testament must be our authority. We can't replace it with ideas of our own.

Susan: I'm sure Professor Lampe would claim his account *is* firmly rooted in the Scriptures. It explains how God was at work in Old Testament times. And it accords with much of what Paul wrote about the need to share in the death of Christ in order to become a new creation - and about the work of the Spirit in making us Christlike (3).

Derek: It occurs to me it's also a fair interpretation of much in the Fourth Gospel, where Jesus repeatedly says his words and actions are not his own but his Father's. Then there are the verses Marion quoted last month, especially where Jesus says 'I and the Father are one.' If Jesus was completely open to God, God could work through him and reveal himself in a human life.

Marion: I'm not completely convinced by all this. Both St. John and St. Paul - since you're appealing to them - say that Jesus existed as the Son before he came to earth. The Word was God from the beginning, and became flesh when Jesus was born. How does Professor Lampe explain that?

Hilda: I was wondering about that. What is there left to celebrate at Christmas if God didn't come to earth in the form of Jesus? The idea that the Spirit of God united with the human spirit of Jesus is all very well, but it seems to take the heart out of the Christmas message.

Susan: I can't answer for Professor Lampe. But several scholars question whether the idea of pre-existence should be taken literally. Have there always been two separate centres of consciousness in heaven, two distinct beings - the Father and the Son - or is this language symbolic? We could interpret the New Testament to mean that Jesus as the Son or the Word was the full expression of God's nature and purpose.

Derek: Some day we'll have to tackle the doctrine of the Trinity! Even if the Son didn't exist as a separate being *before* the lifetime of Jesus, most of us believe that the glorified Jesus is now with the Father. But we'd better leave that issue for another time. What about Hilda's question? What *does* become of Christmas if the pre-existence of the Son is not taken literally?

George: I understand you've already discussed the birth stories. Personally, I find it very difficult to take them literally. Don't they express the importance of Jesus in a poetic way? We can still celebrate his official birthday, and give thanks for what Jesus *became* as he grew up.

Derek: Does that satisfy you, Hilda - thinking of what Jesus came to mean for millions of believers?

Hilda: No, I don't think it does. The Christmas message is that God *came down* to be with us. He crossed the gulf which separated us. Because of his love he took a wonderful initiative to enter human life. What we've heard this evening doesn't seem to contain that joyful news.

Frank: I can see what Hilda means. But isn't it even more wonderful to think of God always seeking to be with us? I've been thinking about one thing said earlier, about God in every age trying to get a personal response from men and women. That appeals to me - the thought of God has been active in ways we've never imagined.

Derek: An interesting thought. But to get back to our understanding of Jesus... Does Professor Lampe's account assume that God had to wait until a man came along who was completely open to him? Was God dependent, in other words, upon Jesus' human response? I can see that

God took a great initiative through Jesus from the moment Jesus accepted his calling, but what if he had refused? What if he had taken a decision that was not in accord with his Father's will?

Susan: I don't see how we can possibly answer that question. It's one of the 'ifs' of history. But if we believe in the full humanity of Jesus, we must assume he had a human mind *and* a human will. It was this self-will that Jesus surrendered. I believe his Messiahship, his role as God's representative, depended on that. He revealed God because he became transparent to God. That's how I see it.

Derek: Thank you for your help this evening, Susan. Once again we've had to ask our brains to work overtime! At least, we can now appreciate that scholars are not trying to undermine the faith of simple believers. The search for understanding must go on. I feel I ought to underline one thing Susan said at the outset. Scholars like Professor Lampe are proposing *alternative* ways of approaching Christian truth, ways which they hope might prove helpful. All religious language is picture language, and a picture which means little to one Christian may help another. We don't see things in the same way.

I've no doubt we'll find this to be the case when we discuss the atonement, the saving work of Jesus. I'm sure Arthur Wilkins will be an understanding guide.

(1) Published by OUP 1977 and by SCM 1983

(2) Op. cit., p.13

(3) See, for example, 2 Corinthians 3 v.17-18 and 5 v.15-17

Comment

Susan omits to mention that Professor Lampe argues not only against the pre-existence of Christ but also against his 'post-existence'. Resurrection, he suggests, 'is the liberation of the life of the individual Jesus to become the life of all men whom God's Spirit...refashions according to his likeness' (op.cit., p.157). The Spirit that was in Christ has been 'let loose in the world'.

Many Christians would want to question this, for they envisage Christ as a glorified human personality radiating light and energy throughout the universe. He is a personal presence who, so they would claim, can still be encountered.

17

The Atonement

Preliminaries: 2 Corinthians 5 v.11 to 6 v.2 and 'Christ is the world's Redeemer' (H&Ps 219).

Derek: We give a warm welcome this evening to the Reverend Arthur Wilkins, who insists we call him Arthur! Welcome to the Thursday Group, Arthur.

Arthur: I hope you're not going to look upon me as the fount of all wisdom. I regard myself as a fellow pilgrim like yourselves.

Derek has asked me to talk about the atonement. Let's start with what Paul said in our reading about the work of reconciliation. That's really what atonement *is*, bringing together two parties who have become estranged.

God and man are estranged. Why is this? Many Christians would say it's because of sin and the guilt attaching to it. But there are other possible reasons. Many people fear God because of ignorance or misunderstanding. Others may resent God because of the way they believe he has treated them.

Paul says, 'God was in Christ reconciling the world to himself.' Yes, but how? That's what the various theories of the atonement seek to explain. For example, some New Testament writers use the category of sacrifice. Many of our Passiontide hymns speak of the death of Christ as an offering for sin. How far is this way of thinking helpful today?

There have been many theories of the atonement. Some are now only of historical interest. Others can still shed light on the mystery. But there is no *official* doctrine. Atonement is first of all a fact of Christian experience. We *know* that through Christ we enjoy an ever-deepening fellowship with the Father. That is the fact we proclaim. How we explain it is of secondary importance.

Well, I hope that's given you enough to start you talking...

Derek: Thank you, Arthur. Are there any immediate reactions?

Norman: I was surprised to hear you say, Mr. Wilkins - Arthur - it may no longer be helpful to think of Jesus' death as an offering for sin. I thought that was central to our faith. Jesus died for the sins of the world. As the hymn says, 'There was no other good enough to pay the price of sin.'

Arthur: I don't want to question deeply-held convictions. Of course there was a strong element of sacrifice in the life of Jesus. Throughout his life he had to sacrifice his own will and desires. He was 'obedient unto death'. But I'm not sure we need interpret the death of Jesus in terms of the Old Testament sacrificial system.

Derek: I think you'll have to spell this out a little more fully, Arthur, now the subject's been mentioned. Most churchgoers assume Jesus died as a sacrifice for sin. Most of us here were probably brought up to believe that, and Charles Wesley's hymns are always reminding us of it!

Arthur: I appreciate the emotional power of such hymns, and of this whole way of thinking about Jesus. I was brought up in the same spiritual atmosphere myself. But over the years I've begun to wonder how far this stands up as a theory of atonement. You see, the whole sacrificial system rested on a premise, an unquestioned assumption, which looks very doubtful today. It's stated in the Epistle to the Hebrews: 'Without the shedding of blood there is no forgiveness' (1). I'm inclined to ask, 'Why not?'

Marion: But since this principle is in the Bible, surely we must accept it. If I may say so, you seem to be questioning one of the foundation stones of the Christian faith. Didn't Jesus himself see his death as an offering for sin?

Arthur: It's possible he did, yes. On the other hand, Our Lord's words at the Last Supper suggest he may have been thinking of a new covenant sealed with his life-blood. It's not easy to know what Jesus' motives were.

Susan: I assume we've been talking about a 'penal substitution' theory of the atonement, where we suppose Jesus bore the punishment due to us. Doesn't this suggest Jesus did something to change God's attitude towards us? Why did God need to see his Son die before he could forgive us?

Marion: Because there was a price to be paid, and Jesus volunteered to pay it on our behalf. He died in our stead.

Susan: But how did this change the situation, Marion? What was the price that had to be paid?

Marion: There's a moral law in the universe that God has to maintain. 'The wages of sin are death.' Our penalty was transferred to Jesus, who was 'made sin' on our behalf.

George: Isn't there something odd about all this—if Marion will excuse me saying so? Jesus was innocent; he was sinless. So his death was an act of injustice. How can any moral law be satisfied by an act of injustice, by punishing the wrong person? It doesn't make sense—not to me, at any rate.

Esther: I believe the death of Jesus shows God's love for us. God has to take the first step, because we were unable to help ourselves. For me, the cross reveals how much God loves us.

Susan: I agree with that, of course. But some of these traditional theories seem to give God a split personality. He loves us and wants to forgive us, but the part of him responsible for the moral law holds him back. The full penalty for all the world's sins has to be paid first.

Arthur: If I can break in here... You're obviously capable of thinking through these issues for yourselves. Perhaps I could urge you to consider another related question. What *is* it that causes estrangement between God and ourselves?

Hilda: I don't understand all this business about satisfying a moral law. To me it's a much more personal matter. I know God has rights over me, but I often want to go my own way. I'm too selfish and wilful. And when I do try to please him, I find I'm too weak to do so. I do not do the good I want to do, as St. Paul says somewhere. All this makes me feel guilty and unworthy.

Arthur: So what you need, Hilda, is an assurance that God accepts you just as you are, in spite of all your weaknesses and failings?

Hilda: I suppose so, yes.

Arthur: May I suggest that if such an assurance is given, and accepted, then atonement has been made as far as you are concerned. There is no longer any barrier; you can approach your Maker without shame or fear.

Derek: Wouldn't some Christians say, Arthur, that there's still the barrier of God's holiness? How can 'polluted mortals', as one hymn calls us, have fellowship with a Being who is morally perfect and aflame with righteousness?

Arthur: I don't see that as a problem. God, if the Old Testament is to be believed, has always sought fellowship with his children. The barriers have all been on the human side.

Gillian: I'm not sure I've got this right, so please correct me if I've misunderstood you. You seem to be saying that God needs to remove certain barriers in *human* hearts and minds. This is what the work of atonement involves. Somehow through what Jesus has done these human barriers are being removed. Is that right?

Arthur: How would others answer that question? As I warned you at the outset, I don't claim to have all the solutions. I certainly think the barriers on the human side are very important - misunderstanding and fear, shame and a sense of guilt, our own wilfulness, and even resentment against God.

Frank: In the Gospels Jesus often give sinners a fresh start, and said how much God rejoiced when one sinner repented. I sometimes think we've made Christianity too complicated with all our theories. Like Esther said earlier, I see the cross as a demonstration of God's love for us. It shows to what lengths God will go to win us back.

Arthur: That's a very important point. God was 'in Christ' even on the cross. To my mind, theories that place Jesus and God on opposite sides in some kind of transaction are seriously misleading.

Derek: So we have arrived at the idea that God was revealing *himself* on the cross, revealing his own attitude towards us, his inexhaustible love.

Arthur: And showing his willingness to absorb the worst that human beings can do, to bear the full brunt of moral evil. The story of the cross has always brought men and women to penitence and wonder. If I may leave you with one last thought... It has been said that the cross revealed, in a moment of time, what is always true within the life of God. God is affected by human sin; our wilfulness causes him anguish. Yet the cross is also, as Thomas Kelly said, 'the measure and the pledge of love' [(2)]. That's why the cross has such power.

Derek: Thank you very much, Arthur. You've certainly given us much to ponder. Of course, there are many atonement theories we haven't mentioned this evening...

Arthur: We can't survey the whole field in thirty minutes. I wouldn't discourage anybody from studying the traditional theories. Many contain insights we can profit from. But we've been trying to concentrate on the essentials. Why is it we are able to approach the throne of grace with boldness? What has made this possible? These are questions we must all answer as best we can.

(1) Hebrews 9 v.22
(2) 'We sing the praise of Him who died' (HAP 182)

Comment

There have been many attempts to construct a satisfying doctrine of the atonement. One of the most enduring has been the theory of 'penal substitution' whereby Christ was punished in man's stead to satisfy the demands of divine justice. This theory is associated with the biblical concepts of ransom and sacrifice. Its classic expression was in the *Cur Deus Homo*? (Why did God become man?) by Anselm written about 1097.

Another type of theory derives from Abelard, a near contemporary of Anselm. For him the cross was a demonstration of God's love which calls forth our repentance. This leads to our forgiveness. The main criticism of this theory is that it does less than justice to the many statements made about the meaning of the cross in the New Testament.

A third approach to the atonement, sometimes referred to as the 'classic theory', speaks of God's victory through the cross over the powers of evil in the world. The cross is seen as a symbol of triumph:

> 'The strife is o'er, the battle done;
> Now is the Victor's triumph won . . .'

Each theory draws attention to some vital aspect of Christ's work, but none is completely satisfying in itself. Anyone interested in pursuing this subject could begin with Chapter 2 of Frances Young's *Can These Dry Bones Live?* (SCM 1982).

18
The Resurrection

Preliminaries: 1 Corinthians 15 v.1-11 and 'Christ is alive! Let Christians sing' (H&Ps 190).

Derek: 'On the third day he rose again.' That's all the Apostles' Creed says about the resurrection. But arguments about the precise nature of this event continue to rage. I knew the name of David Jenkins, the Bishop of Durham, would come up this evening, so I've been trying to find out what he actually said which caused such controversy. Apparently he was on a Radio 4 programme back in 1984, and he remarked that the resurrection was far more than 'a conjuring trick with bones'. In other words, he questioned the idea that the flesh-and-blood body of Jesus was simply brought back to life. To put it crudely, the risen Jesus was not a resuscitated corpse. What, then? Was his body completely transformed in some way we cannot imagine? If so, what kind of experience did the disciples really have in the weeks following the crucifixion?

Then there's the question of evidence. Here we can get some help from this booklet. It's *A Catechism for the use of the people called Methodists* published by the Methodist Publishing House. Let me read one paragraph to you. I quote: 'The evidence for the resurrection is the record, in the New Testament, of the testimony of those who were eyewitnesses of the resurrection; the testimony of those who have experienced him as a living presence throughout the history of the Church; and our own experience of his presence.' There is much for us to ponder there. Where shall we start?

Gillian: To deal with the Bishop of Durham first, I'm sure most Christians believe it *was* the flesh-and-blood body of Jesus that was raised. The tomb was found empty; the body had disappeared. What other explanation could there be?

Linda: Then there's the stories in the Gospels. In the upper room Jesus asked for food, and ate it while the disciples watched. He invited Thomas to touch the wounds in his body. These stories give the impression Jesus has a solid body.

Hilda: But is it quite as simple as that? The Lord suddenly appeared after the disciples had locked the door. He had the power and appear and disappear at will. His body must have been different in some ways.

Derek: I also find it significant that Jesus wasn't always recognized straight away. And some followers, according to Matthew's Gospel, remained in doubt [(1)].

Susan: There's a possibility that Luke and John had their own reasons for stressing the physical nature of Jesus' body. Derek's not the only one who's been doing a bit of research! I've been looking at the Pelican Commentary on Saint Luke's Gospel. It's suggested there that both Luke and John were trying to combat Docetism. According to that heresy, the divine Christ withdrew from the human Jesus before the crucifixion. Apparently that was a widespread belief when these Gospels were written [(2)].

Gillian: I don't quite see the point of that, Susan. Could you explain?

Susan: Well, the belief was that the divine Christ descended upon the man Jesus at his baptism, and then returned to heaven before Jesus was put to death. Luke and John wanted to insist this was wrong. The risen Lord was the same Jesus the disciples had known in the flesh. He wasn't a spirit appearing from heaven.

Derek: What are you implying, then? That the details about Jesus eating food, and inviting Thomas to touch him, were added in the interests of sound doctrine? I'm glad Marion's not here this evening to hear you say that! Most Christians take these stories quite literally.

Hilda: I must say I've never questioned their accuracy. Is there any reason to think they're not entirely trustworthy?

Susan: There is, yes. Think of what Paul said in that passage we read earlier. Remember that was written long before any of the stories in the Gospels. In fact, it's the earliest written evidence we have for the resurrection. Paul lists the appearances of Jesus to the disciples, and doesn't hesitate to add his own experience on the road to Damascus. He doesn't suggest his vision was any different from what the other disciples had experienced.

Derek: Couldn't that be a piece of special pleading? Paul was touchy about his status as an apostle. He wanted to be accepted as the equal of the others.

Susan: But what he says later in the chapter is also significant. 'Flesh and blood can never possess the kingdom of God.' He makes a clear distinction between the earthly animal body we now have and the heavenly spiritual body we shall have after the general resurrection. We will experience a complete transformation.

Derek: What do the rest of you think? If Susan is right, we seem to have conflicting testimony - with Paul on the one hand, Luke and John on the other.

George: Some time ago I read a Saturday Meditation in *The Daily Telegraph* by Bishop George Appleton. According to him, the resurrection appearances were 'a breakthrough from the supernatural.' That phrase stuck in my mind. If Paul's vision was of that kind, perhaps the earlier appearances were too.

Frank: What are we saying, then? That the first disciples had visions, which were 'written up' at a later stage to combat heresy? Is that what it comes to?

Linda: I'll continue to believe the Gospels give us an accurate account of what actually happened. I don't see how these appearances could have been visions. What about the empty tomb, and the fact that Jesus' body was never found?

Derek: We're obviously not going to agree on this. One book I read argued that we could still believe in the resurrection even if some day the bones of Jesus were discovered in Palestine. I was shocked at first, but I can see the point of that remark. It really depends on whether you believe the molecules of Jesus's earthly body were somehow incorporated into his resurrection body. His risen body *could* have been a new creation altogether.

George: That makes sense. What about people whose earthly body is completely destroyed - by cremation, for example? Surely they can still hope for a life beyond death. God must be able to create a different kind of body for them in another medium.

Derek: There's another aspect of this, of course. If Jesus' resurrection body was at least partly physical, what eventually happened to it? We can hardly believe nowadays that it floated up into heaven. However...perhaps we should leave this issue until we discuss the ascension. What about the other kinds of evidence mentioned in the Catechism? That spoke of the experience of Jesus as a living presence, both in the Church and in our own lives.

Hilda: That to me is more important that all this argument about resurrection appearances. 'I know that my Redeemer lives.' That's the heart of our faith, after all.

Derek: If you were talking about your faith to a neighbour, what would you say if she asked *how* Jesus is present in the world today? Christians affirm that Jesus lives. But we think of him going on into another dimension, rather than coming back into this one. How is his presence known here on earth?

Esther: It's an inner experience. Jesus makes himself known to us in our devotional life. What else can we say?

George: Well, I for one can't claim to have spoken to Jesus personally. I might pray to him, although usually I address my prayers to God. I can't honestly swear I've had personal contact with Jesus, in spite of the hymns we're always singing in church. Is that just *me*? Am I the odd one out?

Derek: We respect your honesty, George. Perhaps the devotional tradition we've been brought up in assumes too much. What do you think, Hilda?

Hilda: I've had occasional moments of assurance, but for most of the time I just 'trust and obey'. Jesus *has* been very real to me on a few precious occasions.

Gillian: I find Holy Communion particularly helpful. Jesus did promise, 'This is my body... This is my blood.' I can remember some very powerful Communion services when I've sensed a spiritual Presence with us. Yet at other times it's just been a routine.

Susan: Nothing, as John Betjeman once said,
'Can with this single Truth compare -
That God was Man in Palestine
And lives today in Bread and Wine.'

But to go back to what George said. The Holy Spirit is sometimes thought of as the go-between, or as the other self of Jesus, mediating his blessings to us. So you could argue we 'know Jesus' through our experience of the Spirit. I'm sure there are a lot of Christians like George.

George: Thank you for that! Some of the hymns we sing make me feel I've missed out on something important.

Derek: I'm sure God deals with us as individuals. There's no standard Christian experience we must all conform to. Yet Christ certainly is present in his Church - through his Spirit, if you like. That has been the Church's witness for over nineteen centuries. Perhaps we can take this thought further when we consider the nature of the Church. We have raised more than enough questions for one evening.

(1) Matthew 28 v.17
(2) G.B. Caird, *Saint Luke*, Penguin 1963, p.261

Comment

George Caird, in the commentary cited above, also points out that Jews always thought in concrete terms. Thus it was inevitable that the truth of the resurrection should be expressed in materialistic imagery. On the other hand, describing the resurrection appearances as visions may suggest too subjective an experience. These were, after all, personal encounters. Perhaps the terms '*objective* visions' or 'supernatural encounters' would be more appropriate. According to Wolfhart Pannenberg, 'the appearances of the risen Jesus were experienced as happenings sent from heaven' (*The Apostles' Creed*, SCM 1972, p.116).

With regard to the point made by Susan towards the end of the discussion, William Barclay once wrote: 'To be honest, I find it very difficult to distinguish between the Holy Spirit and the ever present Risen Lord' (*Testament of Faith*, Mowbray 1975, p.109).

19
At God's Right Hand

Preliminaries: Acts 1 v.1-11 and 'Look, ye saints, the sight is glorious' (H&Ps 201).

Derek: We're concerned this evening with two phrases in the Apostles' Creed. We affirm that Jesus 'ascended into heaven' and that he is 'seated at the right hand of the Father'.

One thing that needs interpreting is this movement upwards. People in biblical times believed in a three-decker universe, with heaven literally above the firmament and an underworld beneath their feet. What meaning can such language have today?

The ascension was briefly mentioned last month in connection with the resurrection body of Jesus. Did Luke construct this story in order to remove Jesus' body from the earth? What would you say about that, Susan?

Susan: Luke did have a problem, and his story of the ascension may have been his attempt to solve it. I suspect his story at the beginning of Acts contains more theological teaching than historical fact.

Marion: Trust you to say that, Susan! Why shouldn't the story be true? There were plenty of eye-witnesses who saw and heard what happened.

I can see the idea of Jesus floating upwards *is* a bit strange. Perhaps Jesus just disappeared. The important thing is that he returned to heaven. He wasn't seen again after this - except by Paul on the road to Damascus.

Susan: I don't think the ascension was a separate event at all - separate from the resurrection, I mean. I liked the phrase George quoted last month, where the resurrection appearances were called 'breakthroughs from the supernatural.' Jesus was already *in* the spiritual realm from the moment he was raised from the dead. He broke through from that dimension when he appeared to the disciples.

Linda: What about Luke's order of events, Susan - the resurrection, then the forty days, then the ascension? Did Luke make that up too?

Marion: If he did, the Christian calendar has been wrong for nineteen centuries!

Susan: Does that really matter? We can still celebrate the truth embodied in the story on Ascension Day, even if Luke's account *isn't* historical.

Derek: We're obviously not going to agree about this. So let's turn to the theological truth embodied in the story. Let me refer to a hymn by Charles Wesley which begins 'Entered the holy place above.' It was number 232 in the old Methodist book, but it was omitted from *Hymns and Psalms*. Jesus is first pictured as our great High-priest who 'pleads His passion on the tree' and 'shows Himself to God for me.' In the second verse Jesus becomes our Friend and Advocate whom 'the Father always hears.' In the final verse Jesus is described as our Forerunner with whom our spirit will one day stand.

Does any of this imagery speak to us today? Does it help us to understand the inner meaning of the ascension?

Gillian: I'm afraid I don't know that hymn. Why isn't it in *Hymns and Psalms*? Is there something wrong with its theology? I like the thought of Jesus representing me before God's throne, pleading for me.

Frank: Doesn't that suggest Jesus is trying to make God change his mind about us? It's as though God is a stern Judge, and Jesus is urging him to be lenient.

Derek: We did agree, when we were talking about the atonement, that God and Jesus should not be placed on opposite sides. Some of the hymn's imagery seems to be doing just that. Yes, Esther? You look as though you would like to say something.

Esther: It's just that I like the thought of Jesus as our Forerunner. Jesus told his disciples he was going ahead to prepare a place for them. I think that's a wonderful idea - that Jesus has gone on to heaven and is waiting to welcome us.

Susan: That's true, Esther. But doesn't the image mean more than that? It suggests Jesus has made it *possible* for us to enjoy the life of heaven. By his life of perfect obedience, he has pioneered the way and opened up new possibilities for us.

Gillian: I'm still thinking of Jesus as our High-priest. I thought a priest is a kind of go-between, someone who bridges the gulf between God and ourselves. Surely Jesus can be regarded in that way, as representing us before God.

Derek: We could complete that idea, and say that Jesus also represents God to us. He is 'God for us'. He is the supreme Bridge-builder, at the same time our Representative and God's Representative! I find that idea very helpful.

However... let's move on. One thing I noticed when choosing a hymn to sing this evening was the note of triumph so often struck in verses about the ascension. Christ has triumphed over death and evil; his enemies are in disarray. Or as the popular slogan has it, 'Jesus rules!' He is enthroned in the heights. Perhaps we could consider what we understand by this.

George: I don't want to suggest there's nothing to celebrate, but you must admit there's little evidence that Jesus rules in the world today. I assume the emphasis is on the future. One day Jesus *will* rule on earth. I don't see there's any way he's ruling already - except in heaven, of course.

Norman: Surely we should celebrate our Lord's victory over sin and evil, and over death. He *has* conquered. The victory is his.

Susan: There must be a way in which we can combine these points of view.Both George and Norman are right in what they affirm. When I think of Jesus being enthroned, sitting at God's right hand, I think of him being vindicated. God has acknowledged him. Jesus was not an idealist out of touch with reality, not an impractical dreamer, or a tragic failure. He has been proved right. His teaching, his values, his way of life, have been vindicated. This is the way the world *is*, in spite of appearances to the contrary. The resurrection and ascension are God's 'Yes' to Jesus.

Frank: What about George's point? Many people haven't woken up to the truth of what you're saying. For them Jesus *doesn't* rule.

Hilda: But one day they will realize the truth. I don't believe Jesus will impose his rule on people against their will. Yet there must come a time when they will have to adjust to things as they really are. Don't you think so?

Derek: I'm sure you're right, Hilda. So whey we say 'Jesus rules!' we mean a number of interrelated things. Jesus has been vindicated; he shares God's authority over the universe; even now he is honoured in heaven; he rules on earth in the lives of Christians who are obedient to him; one day he will rule universally. Does that cover it?

Gillian: That sounds pretty comprehensive. We trust that one day everyone *will* acknowledge Jesus as Lord, although - like Hilda - I find it difficult to believe Jesus will ever *impose* his rule by force.

Norman: I'm not sure if *everybody* will accept Jesus as King. There may be some people who will never submit to him. What will become of them?

Derek: We will need to face that issue when we talk about the Last Things - the Second Coming and the Day of Judgment - in our next session. Is there anything more needs to be said about the ascension?

Frank: I'm still a little puzzled about the idea of Jesus moving upwards. I know heaven isn't literally above the clouds, or somewhere beyond the Milky Way. But height is still a powerful symbol. I can't get it out of my mind altogether. You've asked us to imagine Jesus moving into another dimension. But doesn't the idea of height convey something important?

Derek: That's a good point, Frank. We've really said nothing about this symbolism. Can you help us here, Susan?

Susan: Height seems to be a universal symbol. I mean, most religions have imagined the gods living somewhere in the sky. I suppose it suggests the idea of a higher order of existence, free of all earthly limitations. Isn't there also a hint of inaccessibility? The gods are difficult to approach. They must take the initiative in coming down to consort with mortals.

Hilda: We often read in the Bible that God is 'high and lifted up'. Even if we no longer believe in a three-decker universe, as you call it, these expressions still give us a sense of reverence and awe. God is 'nearer to us than breathing', but he is also infinitely greater than us. It does us no harm to think of God and his Christ enthroned 'in the heights'.

Derek: Thank you, Hilda. There's obviously a lot more in the ascension story than we'd previously supposed. I'm sure there's a lot more could be said. But we must leave it there for the moment. Our next discussion will probably take up some of the themes we've touched on this evening.

Comment

John Robinson called the doctrine of the ascension the most *political* of all Christian doctrines, in the sense that it asserts Jesus' right to authority over *every* sphere of life. He continued: 'The doctrine of the Ascension is the assertion of the absolute sovereignty of Jesus over every part of this universe, the crowning of the cross, the manifest triumph of his way of love over every other force in the world' (*But that I can't believe*, Fontana 1967, p.79).

Thus Ascension Day is a yearly reminder to the Church of its function in the world, to bring all men and women and every department of life under the obedience of Christ. It is a festival at which the notes of triumph and acclamation should be blended with those of rededication and mission.

20

THE DAY OF WRATH

Preliminaries: 1 Thessalonians 4 v.13 to 5 v.11 and 'Thou Judge of quick and dead' (H&Ps 247).

Derek: The Apostles' Creed says: 'He will come again to judge the living and the dead.' Let me read to you extracts from the *Dies Irae*, the Day of Wrath. This is part of the Mass for the Dead in the Roman Catholic Church. There was a translation of the Latin words in *The Methodist Hymn Book*, number 646. It begins like this:

'Day of wrath! O day of mourning!
See fulfilled the prophet's warning,
Heaven and earth to ashes burning.
O what fear man's bosom rendeth,
When from heaven the Judge descendeth,
On whose sentence all dependeth.'

The next verse talks about the trumpet sounding, and everyone being brought from their tomb to stand before the throne. Then it goes on:

'Lo! The Book, exactly worded,
Wherein all hath been recorded;
Thence shall judgement be awarded.
When the Judge His seat attaineth
And each hidden deed arraigneth,
Nothing unavenged remaineth.'

This text, dating from the thirteenth century, certainly expresses the traditional belief about the Last Judgment. I'm sure many Christians still imagine it happening in such a way. How do you react to this picture?

Gillian: Isn't it an example of how the Church used to rule by fear? People were scared into obedience. It reminds me of a sampler which once hung on my Grandmother's wall: 'God sees all'. We won't get away with anything; we'll have to pay for every mistake. It's a frightening thought.

Frank: Who is the Judge here? Is it God or Jesus?

Derek: The Judge is Christ himself. A scene of the Last Judgment was often painted on the chancel arch of parish churches. I've seen one in Salisbury. Christ is enthroned in the centre. The heavenly city is on the left hand side, and the torments of hell on the right. Sometimes people are shown emerging from their tomb to meet their fate.

Marion: Surely *we* don't need to worry about the Judgment. St. Paul says in the passage we read this evening that God has destined us to salvation. If we have faith in Jesus we have nothing to fear. It's the worldly-minded and the unbelievers who need to be warned.

Susan: I can't help feeling there's something basically wrong about the picture of Christ in the *Dies Irae*. Is this the same Jesus we read about in the Gospels, who was full of compassion and who assured sinners of God's mercy? What happened to that Jesus?

Norman: Jesus also had hard things to say about people who rejected him. Several verses in the Gospels speak of eternal punishment, of wailing and gnashing of teeth, of the fire reserved for the Devil and his followers. Jesus gives us a choice, and if we decide against him we must accept the consequences.

Frank: Are we meant to take this pictures literally? They don't seem to fit very well with the belief that God is love.

Marion: But St. Paul also had a lot to say about the wrath of God. I don't think we can ignore God's horror of sin. Some of us seem to forget this side of God's nature.

Derek: That's true. Perhaps you could explain your views about this, Susan. In objecting to the idea of a Judgment, are you playing down the reality of sin?

Susan: I don't deny the reality of judgment, although I'm not so sure about the idea of a once-and-for-all *Final* Judgment. To take up Frank's point, I believe God is always motivated by love - even in judgment. Sometimes Christians have projected their own human feelings onto God, especially a certain vindictiveness against their enemies. I think the author of Revelation is guilty of this, as are all Christians who have dwelt on the terrors of hell with relish.

Gillian: How do you suppose God judges in a loving way, Susan?

Susan: Well, a person who lives a selfish or wicked life is destroying himself spiritually. We all agree on that. Surely God would want to point out the consequences of such a life, and to destroy any illusions - in other words, to bring people to recognize spiritual realities.

Marion: But, Susan, these people have the Bible. They have the teaching of the Church. They have their own God-given conscience. If they choose to ignore all this, they've only got themselves to blame.

Hilda: If I can interrupt this argument for a minute! I've thought of something that might support Susan, at least on the last point she made. Some time ago a friend lent me a book about near-death experiences. I think the author was a man called Raymond Moody. Some of the people he interviewed claimed they had seen flashbacks of their earlier life, with a voice asking questions about how they had behaved. I thought when I read it what a loving way that would be for God to deal with us. We would have to face our faults and be given a chance to learn from them.

Marion: You mean everybody would be given another chance to repent? Surely it's in *this* life we have to make the decisions that matter.

Gillian: I'm not sure that can be the whole story, Marion. What about people who have never heard the gospel preached clearly, or those whose character has been warped by their upbringing? Surely men and women like that deserve a second chance.

Susan: Isn't it a question of what God, as a loving Father, would do? I don't see how he could abandon any of his children without trying time and time again to win a response from them.

Norman: But don't you think, Susan, there may be people who reject God, and all he has to offer, once and for all? Then God would have to leave them alone.

Susan: You may be right. But remember what Jesus taught about our willingness to forgive. 'Seventy times seven' means 'without limit'. What applies to us must surely apply to God himself. Although I admit that forgiveness - to be effective - must be accepted. Some might reject God's forgiveness.

Derek: Perhaps we ought to get back to the *Dies Irae*, or at least to the belief in a Second Coming. Is this another credal statement that needs to be reinterpreted, or can we still believe in a dramatic return of Christ to earth? What do you think, Hilda?

Hilda: Human history has got to end sometime. But I find it hard to imagine Jesus actually appearing in the clouds and descending to earth. Where would he land? It was alright to believe as Paul did while it was thought the earth was flat - but not nowadays.

Susan: There are millions of fundamentalists, all over the world, who *do* still take this New Testament picture literally. They speak about the Rapture when they believe they will be caught up to meet Christ in the air.

Norman: This *is* the picture St. Paul gives us. If we're going to explain it away, what do we put in its place?

Susan: There's no doubt the first generation of Christians did expect Jesus to return during their lifetime. That expectation has been renewed at regular intervals. But I believe Jesus is returning all the time into believers' lives, through the Spirit.

Linda: But there must come a time when everyone will have to recognize Christ's authority, when he really does become King over the whole human race.

Derek: I've been looking up what the Methodist Catechism says about this. I quote: 'Question 61. What do the Creeds teach about the second coming of Jesus and the final judgement? In his own way and in his own time God will finally judge the human race through Christ, bring all things together under the authority of Christ, and establish his reign of love for ever.' I assume we can all agree with that?

George: I like the bit about 'in his own way and in his own time'. It's the kind of statement world leaders make after a summit meeting to cover up their differences. It could mean anything!

Derek: Isn't that the best way to leave it, George? We all agree on the basic principles. We're faced with the usual question of how far we take the images in the Bible literally. Most New Testament scholars seem to agree that Jewish prophecies about the Day of the Lord - when God would destroy his enemies and establish his rule - were applied to Jesus. We must seek the truth behind the pictures, the kernel within the shell. I think the Catechism expresses this very well.

Marion: I don't know if I'm in a minority of one, but I still think Jesus *will* return in glory. There must be a definite end to history, a moment when this present order is replaced. It will be the End with a capital 'E'. How this will happen I can't really imagine. But everyone *will* have to acknowledge Jesus as Lord and King. I'm quite certain about that.

Derek: For once we'll let Marion have the last word! Thank you all for your thoughts on this topic.

Comment

In contrast to the millions of fundamentalist Christians throughout the world who are expecting a literal fulfilment of 1 Thessalonians 4 v.15-17 in the near future, some liberal Christians reinterpret the doctrine in terms of individual experience. Thus William Barclay suggests that we are to think of the Second Coming 'not as one single event, but as an infinitely repeated event in the soul of each individual man' (*The Plain Man Looks at the Apostles' Creed*, Fontana 1967, p.197). But it is questionable whether a dramatic finale to God's purposes in Christ can be denied altogether. Both Old and New Testaments speak of a consummation of history when final judgments are pronounced.

Teaching that God consigns unrepentant sinners to the torments of hell has provoked moral outrage, yet it can be argued that we inflict these torments on ourselves by refusing to love or to respond to God's love. If human beings are genuinely free, the possibility of an eternal rejection of love must remain open. Do such souls cease to exist, or does God never admit defeat in the case of a single soul? The 'hard sayings' of Jesus about outer darkness should deter us from taking too sentimental a view of divine love.

21
A Committee of Three?

Preliminaries: Ephesians 1 v.3-14 and 'Born by the Holy Spirit's breath' (H&Ps 279).

Derek: I have arranged for some moral support this evening! I've asked a few of the group to choose a hymn about the Holy Spirit and to be prepared to comment on it. First of all I'll say something about the place of the Holy Spirit in the Trinity. I asked Andrew for help with this, and he has lent me a book by Keith Ward, a Professor at King's College, London. On the front cover Professor Ward is described as a 'champion of the Faith', although I believe his most recent book is far from orthodox. However, the volume I have here obviously meets with our minister's approval!

The book is called *The Living God*. I've made a note of a few points from the final chapter, which is about the Trinity. First, he says that the original word translated 'persons' was never intended to mean separate personalities. We shouldn't imagine an endless committee meeting! Rather, we must think of God under three aspects or images. These are complementary but distinct. When we speak of God as Father, we think of him as the one who orders the universe, and who is guiding it towards goodness. God as Son is the way God has shown himself to us in time and space, revealing his character in a particular form. God as Spirit is - and I quote - 'God working to redeem humanity through his presence within our hears and minds' (1).

So the Holy Spirit isn't to be thought of as a kind of impersonal energy. He is God himself active in human life, equipping his servants and transforming their nature.

I don't know if anyone would like to make a comment on that summary? Most of the things we want to say about the Holy Spirit will emerge when we talk about the hymns you've chosen

Susan: That sounds like a very helpful summary of the doctrine of the Trinity. I can recall a phrase of Karl Barth's - 'God in his three ways of being God'. I like the way you spoke of God *as* Father, *as* Son, and *as* Spirit. These are the three ways God has revealed himself to us.

Derek: Good. Now let's see if my volunteers are prepared. In *Hymns and Psalms* the 'Eternal Spirit' section is subdivided into 'The Giver of Life', 'In the Church', and 'For the World'. Has anyone chosen a hymn from the first subsection? I suggest we find whatever hymn is mentioned, and look at it together.

Hilda: Well, I'm very fond of number 281, 'Come down, O Love divine'. I like Vaughan Williams' tune too, but the words are particularly beautiful. Derek mentioned how the Spirit changes our nature. This hymn speaks of Love coming like a flame to burn earthly passions away. I think that's a wonderful idea.

Derek: Thank you, Hilda. The third verse stresses 'true lowliness of heart'. Is that a quality you particularly value?

Hilda: Well, we're told that pride is the worst sin, and lowliness is its opposite. We need to admit our faults and long to have them corrected.

Gillian: That links up with the hymn I've chosen. It's number 312, 'Our blest Redeemer, ere he breathed'. We had a minister once who told us how some well-known hymns were composed. There's a story that Harriet Auber didn't have a pencil and paper handy when the inspiration came, so she scratched the words on a pane of glass with her ring. Anyway... what Hilda said reminded me of verse 5, where 'every virtue we possess, and every victory won' witnesses to the work of the Spirit in our hearts.

George: I see the Spirit is referred to here as coming in tongues of flame, and being like the wind. If the Spirit is God himself, isn't it misleading to use such impersonal images? There's the dove too. The previous hymn talks about the 'heavenly Dove'. It's no wonder Christians often think of the Spirit as a force or energy.

Gillian: But that's not true of all the images used of the Spirit, George. Harriet Auber, in her first verse, calls him our Guide and Comforter. And isn't the Spirit called our Advocate in some hymns?

Linda: This hymn also calls him 'a gracious, willing guest'. I like that idea. A guest who only comes when he's invited! By the way, why does this hymn book call the author Henriette Auber? I thought her name was Harriet.

Derek: I believe the lady was known by both names. But what about George's point? In Christian art the Spirit is often shown as a dove. That must affect people's ideas about the Spirit. According to Keith Ward, some Christians think of the Holy Spirit as a sort of treacle! You get a little at baptism, more at confirmation, and then regular doses at communion.

Frank: I once heard a children's address where the preacher used electricity as an illustration. And another when the Spirit was compared to the hand inside a puppet. Come to think of it, that's a little more personal than electricity!

Derek: It shows that people remember children's addresses, at any rate! Now you have the floor, Frank, perhaps you would like to introduce your hymn.

Frank: I should have kept my mouth shut! But since you ask, I chose number 286, 'Gracious Spirit, dwell with me'. There's little in this hymn that hasn't already been mentioned. I like the way it talks directly to the Spirit, asking him to live within us. It would make a good prayer to use at home. It describes the kind of life we would like to lead every day.

Susan: I agree, Frank. That's an interesting point, about praying *to* the Spirit. Do you ever do that when you're leading worship. Derek?

Derek: I don't find it comes naturally, no. We usually think of approaching God *through* Christ and *in* the Spirit. According to Paul in Romans 8, the Spirit helps us to pray. But since the Spirit *is* God, there's no logical reason why we shouldn't speak to God as Spirit.

We haven't heard your choice yet, Linda. What is your favourite hymn about the Spirit?

Linda: I chose number 301, 'Gracious Spirit, Holy Ghost'. It's based on 1 Corinthians 13 where Paul describes Christian love. I think love is the most important of the Holy Spirit's gifts. The tune fits the words so well, too.

Derek: Thank you, Linda. Are there any more choices from the first two subsections? What about you, Esther?

Esther: I was going to mention number 304, 'Holy Spirit, hear us'. I know it's a children's hymn; it takes me back to my childhood days in Sunday School. It says everything so simply, but it's all there - inspiration when we worship and pray, guidance when we read the Bible, help with becoming more like Jesus and doing what is right. I like reading it through.

Derek: Good. There's virtue in being simple and straightforward. In the time we have left we ought to consider hymns from the 'For the World' subsection. It's not difficult to understand the idea of God as Spirit being active in individual lives, and in the life of the Church. But how is God active in the world at large? Has anyone chosen a hymn between numbers 314 and 328?

Susan: I plead guilty to that! I'm much taken by Michael Hewlett's verses, number 324, beginning:

> 'Sing to him in whom creation
> Found its shape and origin.'

The first verse speaks of God as Spirit being the life 'in whom all lives begin'. The second verse reminds us how close God is to all his children, speaking to them through the voice of conscience. But it's the third verse I like the best:

'His the truth behind the wisdoms
Which as yet know not our Lord...'

This suggests God as Spirit has inspired what is true in other religions and philosophies. Some Christian theology hasn't really come to terms with that idea.

The remaining verses follow more familiar lines, although the last verse has an interesting phrase about the Trinity.The three aspects of God are described as 'Source, and Truth, and Inspiration'.

Derek: Thank you, Susan. That's a hymn we can read through more carefully at home. Did you want to add something, George?

George: Only that my own choice, another modern hymn, seems to cover similar ground in fewer words. It's number 290 by Ann Phillips, 'Into a world of dark'. It starts with the work of creation, bringing form and shapelessness and a plan from nothing. It ends with God's Spirit giving mankind the pattern of a new life. I like the sense this hymn gives of the whole sweep of history.

Derek: That's another hymn most of us are probably not familiar with. We've time for one more choice. What about yours, Norman?

Norman: I'm surprised nobody's mentioned number 326, which has become very popular - 'There's a spirit in the air'. In two verses God, Christ, and the Spirit are all mentioned. God in Christ has come to stay, and it's the Spirit who now leads us forward.

Derek: Good. You all seem to have enjoyed this excursion into *Hymns and Psalms*. Perhaps we could approach one of the remaining topics in a similar way - not the one about the Church, but the following session about everlasting life.

We would probably need to use the old *Methodist Hymn Book* for that. There's not a great deal about the life to come in *Hymns and Psalms*. I'm sure they have some old books at Notbury we could borrow. Thank you all for your contributions this evening. There's far more we could say about 'the outreach of God', but our time is up.

(1) Keith Ward, *The Living God*, SPCK 1984, p.131

Comment

Leonard Hodgson, sometime Regius Professor of Divinity at Oxford, once remarked that Christianity 'began as a trinitarian religion with a unitarian theology'. The original Jewish Christians were monotheists, but their religious experience led them to *worship* Christ and to recognize the Spirit who constituted them the messianic community as also God. In the next two or three centuries the church sought to answer the question how God could be both One and Three.

Several solutions were rejected, including 'modalism' which conceived of God as a single person who appeared successively in different forms. The *Quicunque Vult*, once attributed to St. Athanasius, appears to consist of a series of contradictions. The real solution, as Professor Hodgson suggested, may be to revise our idea of unity. Man himself is a mysterious creature who exists in three distinct yet interrelated activities - thinking and feeling and willing. God's being is 'incomprehensible', beyond our power to conceive, yet our own experience of the complicated unity of human personality makes it reasonable to suppose that the life of God is infinitely more complex.

22

ONE CHURCH OR MANY?

Preliminaries: 1 Peter 2 v.1-10 and 'Behold the temple of the Lord' (H&Ps 808).

Derek: The Apostles' Creed talks about 'the holy catholic Church', and the Nicene Creed expands this to the 'one holy catholic and apostolic Church'. That's all very well in theory, but the reality seems to be quite different. What we see are many different churches, each with its distinctive doctrines, forms of worship, style of government, and so on. What can the high-sounding phrases in the Creeds possibly mean?

Gillian: We were once taught that 'holy' means belonging to God, set aside for his use - not pious or good in a moral sense. Some people have the idea the church ought to consist of saints rather than sinners. No wonder they're disappointed!

Derek: And what about 'catholic'?

Frank: Nothing to do with the Roman Catholic Church, of course. Doesn't the word mean universal, meant for all people?

Derek: You have obviously been well-instructed! In what sense would you say the church is 'one'?

Marion: Well, as you say, it's obviously not a united organization. Yet we sing about 'one church, one faith, one Lord'. I suppose we're all united with Christ, and therefore with one another through Christ. And we all share in the Spirit. No particular denomination has a monopoly of the Holy Spirit.

Derek: Good. We're off to a flying start this evening! Let me ask you another question. What do you think the church is *for*? What is its reason for existence, its purpose?

Marion: I should have thought that was obvious. The church consists of those who have been saved. God saves everyone who accepts Christ as their Lord. They become united with him, and share the gifts of the Spirit.

Susan: So you think the church exists for the benefit of the people inside it? What about the idea that the church exists mainly for the sake of those who are *outside* its fellowship?

Linda: What do you mean, Susan? That we're called to help save others?

Susan: You could put it that way. The same issue arises in the Old Testament over the vocation of Israel. Why did God have a chosen people? Was it for privilege or for service?

Marion: We've obviously got to witness to what God has done for us. We belong to Christ, and we must persuade others to make the same commitment as we have.

Gillian: Can anyone explain to me what is meant by the Servant Church? It's a phrase we've heard a lot in recent years. Is it a matter of bringing more people to Christ, or are we meant to serve others without trying to convert them? When I've been collecting for Christian Aid, I've met a few committed Christians who are reluctant to contribute. They prefer to support organizations that deliberately set out to make converts.

Frank: Has it got to be one or the other? Lots of medical missionaries witness to their faith through their work. They're commending Christianity by deeds rather than words.

Susan: I think we should see God's purposes in a wider framework. There's a verse in Ephesians 1 that speaks of God bringing all things into a unity in Christ. Doesn't that suggest that *all* aspects of human life must be transformed? I think of the church being called to influence practically everything - politics, international affairs, standards of life in third world countries, and so on. That's what I understand by the phrase Gillian mentioned - the Servant Church.

Derek: Doesn't that link with some of the parables Jesus told, about the kingdom being like yeast working in the dough or like salt which seasons the whole meal? Is that the kind of influence the church should have in the world.

Marion: That's all very well, but witnessing to Jesus Christ is also important. We've got to proclaim him as Lord, and encourage more and more people to share in the work of the kingdom.

Derek: Let's turn to the fact that there are so many different churches and denominations. Is this a serious hindrance to the work of the kingdom - to use Marion's phrase?

George: Won't there always be different approaches to the Christian religion? Last Easter a friend of mine invited me to spend a day at Spring Harvest, in a holiday camp at Minehead. It was interesting, but definitely not my scene. The worship was too emotional for my liking.

Hilda: Yet some Baptist neighbours of mine go every year and think it's marvellous. They say it charges up their batteries for twelve months. I'm not sure I would like to spend a week there, but good luck to those who do find it an inspiration.

Derek: There's a fine sermon by John Wesley called 'Catholic Spirit'. When I meet a fellow Christian, he says, I don't ask him if he shares my opinions, or worships in the same way as I do. All I ask is: 'Is your heart as my heart? If it is, give me your hand.'

Frank: What are we saying, then? That there will always be different churches with distinctive theological viewpoints and styles of worship? Is the uniting of the churches into a single organization ever going to be possible? Or even desirable?

George: Can you imagine a massive church bureaucracy like the European Community has at Brussels? We can do without that! I wouldn't be too happy with a united church centred at Rome either.

Hilda: We've been praying for Christian unity every year in January for as long as I care to remember. Are we now saying it's all been a waste of time?

Derek: Surely not! We've been worshipping together, listening to one another, planning joint ventures and so on. We've been doing exactly what John Wesley urged us to do - praying for one another, encouraging one another, provoking one another to good works. The Spirit has certainly been at work in all this.

Frank: So do we agree there will always be diversity - in theology, organization, worship? Does God will it so - or is that a heretical thought in these ecumenical times?

George: People themselves are so different, and I assume their spiritual needs are different too. I don't feel I've got much in common with a Roman Catholic in Mexico honouring his local saint, or with an evangelist on American television for that matter. They don't share my understanding of the Christian faith.

Gillian: I'm sure God works through all the various churches. The mistake is to think that *our* particular way is the only right one.

Derek: Do any of you remember a paper called *Joyful News*? It used to include advertisements for holiday accommodation, like the *Methodist Recorder* does today. Many of these used to say: 'A special welcome for the Lord's people.' I often wondered who 'the Lord's people' were.

Susan: Obviously people who believed they belonged to an 'in group' which made the rest of the world's population outsiders. There's been far too much bigotry and intolerance in Christian history.

Linda: Isn't that being a little unkind to the readers of this *Joyful News*? They were probably sincere Christian people who had accepted Jesus as their Lord. What's wrong with that?

Derek: What we must condemn is the 'we're completely right, you're completely wrong' attitude. No group or church has a monopoly of the truth. There may always be *some* truth in what the other chap believes!

I'm sure we're in no position to draw a line through the human race and say: 'People on our side of the line are saved; the people on the other side are doomed.'

Gillian: Some churches and sects will get a big surprise in heaven, when they see 'the other lot' there as well! I suppose what we're saying is that only God knows his own.

Derek: That brings us back to where we started. The church can be seen as consisting of those whom God has called to forward his purposes in the world. There are many churches but only one Church in this sense.

Frank: Could the Church thus understood include men and women who aren't members of a church organization at all? I've often wondered about that.

Derek: That's a difficult one, Frank. The Catechism does talk about being called 'through Jesus Christ' and sharing in 'the unity that the Spirit gives'. I can see God might inspire people who have no specific Christian allegiance. One thinks of Mahatma Ghandi, for instance, or of Dag Hammarskjold - a famous Secretary General of the United Nations - who once claimed he had answered Yes to Someone or Something. But can we talk about the Church without reference to Christ?

Susan: There's good biblical precedent for the idea of God working through outsiders, if you can call them that. Cyrus the Persian is called 'the Lord's anointed' (1).

Hilda: Some leaders like Ghandi have been more Christian in spirit than others within the churches who are always going on about Christ. 'By their fruits you shall know them,' our Lord said.

Derek: And that's where we must leave the matter for this evening. We've said nothing about baptism or apostolic succession. I suppose if we wanted to enter the theological minefield of rites of entry and valid orders, we could do so on another occasion. But, thankfully, not now!

(1) Isaiah 45 v.1

Comment

The Methodist Catechism makes a useful distinction between the Church with a capital 'C', which consists of all those called by God through Jesus Christ to be his people, and churches with a small 'c' which are human social institutions. Each church on earth 'shares with all such groups the need to achieve its identity, to protect itself against threats, and to obtain and control power. From New Testament time onwards this had led to conflict, separation and hostility' (*A Catechism for the use of the people called Methodists*, p.24).

The only hope for progress towards realizing the visible unity of the Church on earth is for Christians 'to acknowledge the relativity of all systems of doctrine and forms of ecclesiastical order', so that they may be prepared to follow the Holy Spirit's guidance in a transformation of the churches (A.R. Vidler, *Christian Belief*, SCM p.85).

23
The Life Everlasting

Preliminaries: Revelation 21 v.1-4, 22-27 and 22 v.1-5 and 'Give me the wings of faith to rise' (H&Ps 815).

Derek: 'I believe in the communion of saints...the resurrection of the body, and the life everlasting.' These are the phrases we're considering this evening.

First, let me remind you of a few New Testament passages. On the resurrection of the body we have the teaching of Paul in the second half of 1 Corinthians 15. According to Paul, we shall one day have a spiritual body which is imperishable and immortal. So we can assume we'll be recognized in the life to come, and we'll be able to express ourselves.

With regard to the communion of saints, we have the picture in Hebrews 12 of a cloud of witnesses watching us run 'the race for which we are entered' like spectators at a sporting contest. There are also descriptions in Revelation of the hosts before the heavenly throne.

The nature of the life everlasting is left to the imagination. Some writers have supposed that each individual soul enjoys the 'beatific vision' of God and remains in timeless adoration. But most Christians have imagined a heavenly society in which there is personal interaction, meeting and fellowship.

We decided we would make use of the old *Methodist Hymn Book*, where there are twenty hymns under the heading 'Death, Judgement, the Future Life'. I've chosen five hymns, and given one to each of our volunteers to comment on. We'll deal with these hymns as far as possible in the order in which they were written. That puts you first, Norman.

Norman: I thought it might! Derek gave me number 655, 'Jerusalem, my happy home'. This seems to be based on the final chapters in Revelation. The holy city has walls of precious stones, gates of pearl, streets paved with gold, and so on. There are vineyards and orchards, gardens and flowers of great beauty. There's music in the air, with David acting as choirmaster. The saints see God face to face and spend all their time rejoicing. It's the picture most people have of heaven.

Hilda: I don't think we should dismiss it entirely. People who've had near-death experiences sometimes say they caught a glimpse of beautiful gardens beyond the point they reached.

George: Can we place much reliance on reports like those? It might all be going on in their heads. It's what they *expected* to see. Couldn't they have been dreaming?

Hilda: People who have had these experiences always say it was different from a dream - much more vivid and real. This might be just the kind of reception God *would* provide, to help us adjust to a new life.

Derek: An interesting point. Let's move on to the next hymn, number 647 by Richard Baxter, 'Lord, it belongs not to my care'. What did you make of this one, Esther?

Esther: I thought it was a lovely hymn. The writer doesn't worry whether his life is long or short, because serving the Lord is all that matters. I like the idea of death being a door into rooms that the Lord has already been through. It's enough for him that he'll be with Christ. I should think this hymn would be a comfort to anyone who's worried about death.

Derek: Thank you, Esther. In earlier centuries people were much more conscious of the ever-present threat of death. Now most of us can look forward to a longer life, and death seems to have receded into the distance.

Gillian: That may be one reason why most of these hymns have not been included in *Hymns and Psalms*. We don't often think about the life to come. When did we last hear a sermon on the subject?

Derek: Is this because Christians have lost their faith in life after death, do you think?

George: A lot of people do have doubts about this. It is difficult to see how anything of us can survive when our brain dies. Aren't some writers now saying that the phrase 'eternal life' really means a new quality of life here and now?

Susan: It's certainly a quality of life we can begin to experience now. I came across a good illustration recently which answers your point about the brain. This chap said he has a computer which stores information on discs.Any time he needs it he can reproduce a sheet of facts or figures which is identical to the original sheet. In a similar way, God must know the complete specification of every individual. He has all the details stored in his memory. So he can always recreate a complete person in a new medium, with a 'spiritual body' which resembles our old earthly body.

Derek: That's an illustration worth remembering. I gave our third hymn to Hilda. It's number 649 by Isaac Watts, 'There is a land of pure delight'. This *has* been retained in the new book.

Hilda: I can't say I'm over-fond of this hymn. It talks about 'sweet fields...dressed in living green'. Apart from that, it uses the idea that death is like the River Jordan. We shouldn't hesitate to cross, because Canaan the promised land lies on the other side. The final verse runs:

'Could we but climb where Moses stood,
And view the landscape o'er,
Not Jordan's stream, nor death's cold flood,
Should fright us from the shore!'

All I can say is, whatever God has prepared for us on the other side, I'm sure we won't be disappointed!

Derek: Thank you. Perhaps we should now ask Gillian to introduce number 642. It's by the American poet John Greenleaf Whittier, 'When on my day of life the night is falling'. What did you think of these verses, Gillian?

Gillian: Did you know Whittier is one of my favourite hymn-writers? His verses really speak to me. He expects no 'gate of pearl', nor does he believe he's deserved any palm branch. It will be enough for him if he finds himself beckoned by familiar hands into his fitting place. I'll follow Hilda's example and example and quote the last verse:

'There, from the music round me stealing,
I fain would learn the new and holy song,
And find at last, beneath Thy trees of healing,
The life for which I long.'

Don't we all, in our better moments, long for a life on a higher level? We've caught a glimpse of it on a few precious occasions, and we know it's somewhere beyond us. That's how I feel, at any rate.

Linda: It sounds a very homely kind of hymn. I've always found talk about the holy city and massed choirs rather off-putting, but this is different. We're not lost in a crowd, but surrounded by friends and 'kindly faces'. I find that idea comforting.

Derek: Now we've touched on the communion of saints, perhaps we could move on to Marion's hymn. It's number 657, 'For those we love within the veil', by William Charter Piggott.

Marion: I found this quite thought-provoking. Our friends 'within the veil', it says, are no longer toilworn and burdened with care, but erect and clear-eyed. I thought of that the other evening when I was in the geriatric ward. I was particularly interested in verse 6, where it's suggested the departed may still influence our life here on earth. I'd like to hear what others think about that. *Do* relatives and friends who have died still have an interest in us?

Hilda: I'll tell you what a former deaconess once confided in me. A few days after her husband died she suddenly became aware of his presence in the room. She saw nothing and heard nothing, but she just *knew* he was there. Then the feeling passed. It was as though her husband had come back to assure her all was well. She stopped grieving, and found the courage to get on with her life. I'm sure God allowed her husband to return for that single visit.

Derek: It also suggests the husband knew of his wife's distress... Was there anything else you were going to mention, Marion?

Marion: Well, there's also the idea that there's work to be done in heaven. Verse 4 says:

> 'With quickened sense and heightened joy
> They serve Thee still.'

Then in verse 6 it says God still employs 'their ripened powers' for some higher purpose. I don't understand what this can mean.

Susan: In one of his books C.S. Lewis pictures the Shining Ones talking to visitors from Hell and urging them to stay [(1)]. Think of all the millions of souls who will need counselling in the next life - people who are still earth-bound, and who find it difficult to adjust to the life of heaven. The possibilities are endless.

Derek: I'm sure there will be opportunities for fellowship and further spiritual growth. Heaven has been pictured as a kind of garden suburb with a varied programme of cultural activities. That must be a travesty of the truth, yet there'll surely be scope for personal talents to be developed.

Susan: Paul does say more than once that our experience of the Spirit is a foretaste of the life to come. The Greek word he uses was a commercial term, meaning 'first instalment' or something of the sort [(2)]. So all that we associate with the Spirit gives some indication of what the life of heaven must be like.

Derek: That's a very helpful point with which to end. We can all think through the implications of that for ourselves. Our five volunteers have earned our gratitude. Thank you all.

[(1)] *The Great Divorce*, reprinted as a Found Paperback 1977
[(2)] 2 Corinthians 1 v.22 and Ephesians 1 v.14

Comment

There are some Christian theologians who argue that individual men and women survive death only as memories in God's mind. Thus David Edwards once wrote: 'God will continue to love *you*, the *you* he knows, and *you* will have your own place in the glory of God!' (*Asking Them Questions*, OUP 1973, p.56).

Others suppose that the natural end of man is extinction, but that God will resurrect those who have been faithful to him by an act of divine power. On the other hand, if any reliance can be placed on reports of near-death experiences, then continuing personal existence could be a universal phenomenon. In that case, the Christian concept of resurrection would involve a *spiritual* rebirth, a metamorphosis into a new *quality* of life. Such a process could be conceived as beginning now and finding its fulfilment hereafter.

24
THE CHRISTIAN PILGRIMAGE

Preliminaries: Philippians 3 v.1-14 and 'When our confidence is shaken' (H&Ps 686).

Derek: We give a warm welcome to Arthur on his second visit to us. We're very glad you were able to come, Arthur, and we're looking forward very much to what you have to say.

Arthur: I'm usually rooted to my armchair in the evening. But Derek was very persuasive, so here I am! I've been told I can talk about any aspect of Christian belief. Let me tell you a little about how my own beliefs have changed through the years. Then we'll see what emerges from that.

I was brought up in a strict Methodist home. We all took it for granted that the Bible was literally the word of God. I can't remember having any doubts about that. Then in due course I offered for the ministry... At college we were introduced to the critical approach to the Bible, and I must say I found it hard to come to terms with. I gave the answers I thought were expected, but privately I had my reservations.

However, that was a long time ago. I've become steadily more open-minded as I've grown older. The certainties of youth have become the uncertainties of age! I'll give you one example. Last time I came here we were talking about the atonement. As a young minister I believed implicitly in the idea of penal satisfaction. This was a corner-stone of our evangelical faith. Now I'm not so sure... I can see that as a theory of the atonement it's open to serious objections.

I'm very taken by the hymn of Fred Pratt Green we sang earlier. My experience must be similar to his. There have been times in my own ministry when my confidence has been shaken in beliefs I thought secure. Some theology is too self-confident. It offers easy answers when it would be wiser to stay silent. I believe we must learn to live with unanswered questions.

Perhaps I've said enough by way of introduction. I'll now hand over to Derek...

Derek: Thank you, Arthur. May I take you up on the last point you made? Could you give us an example of a question we cannot answer?

Arthur: Some of us were profoundly shocked when we learnt what had been going on in the death camps - at Auschwitz and Belsen, and elsewhere. Then there were the reports from Hiroshima and Nagasaki after the atomic bombs were dropped. There is a mystery here - the intensity of moral evil in a world God is responsible for, the extremes of human suffering God permits. I don't know how to explain it or to justify it.

Norman: I was interested in your point about theology being too self-confident. Does this apply to the statements of faith in the historic Creeds?

Arthur: That's a difficult one... I think we need to see these Creeds in their context. They were meant to refute heresy, and they belong to the world in which they were produced. There was once a Professor of Divinity - Leonard Hodgson was his name - who used to say to his students: 'What must the truth be now if people who thought as they did put it like that?' That seems to me to be a good question to bear in mind when we approach the Bible and the Creeds.

Derek: In our own amateurish way that's what we have been trying to do. But we haven't always agreed how much freedom we should allow ourselves. Sometimes we've moved a long way from what the Creeds have obviously meant.

Arthur: Have you ever considered the parallel between theology and science? A scientist seeks to discover how things are, and he proposes a theory as a working hypothesis. But if further experiments show this theory is inadequate, it is amended or a new theory is proposed. Scientific statements are always provisional and subject to revision. I sometimes think theology should be conducted in a similar way.

Marion: I'm not very happy with that idea. In theology the truth has been *revealed* to us. It's not something we have had to work out for ourselves.

Arthur: But isn't there a sense in which scientific truth has been revealed to the scientist? Is the process of inspiration so different?

Derek: It's often said that all theological statements are culture-related. The truth has to be expressed within a particular framework of thought, and these frameworks change from one age to another.

Arthur: Indeed. And there has also been a great increase in secular knowledge, knowledge about the world we live in, during the past two hundred years or so. Think how this has affected our ideas about Creation and the Fall, to take but two examples. Theology must interpret the world as it is, not as it was once thought to be.

Hilda: Can I ask you about your ministry in various circuits, Arthur? You say your ideas have changed a good deal over the years. What about the people you've met in the circuits? Have you been able to help them to cope with new ideas?

Arthur: That's a difficult question. I've sometimes asked myself whether I did enough along those lines. Let me make two points in my own defence. I recently heard it said that only four per cent of the adult population can think theologically. Certainly, most of the people in the congregations I faced were not at ease with theological ideas. I found that to be true in the discussion groups I started. Things may be different now. Educational methods have changed. It's become fashionable to question everything.

Then my primary responsibility was a pastoral one. I still believe it is wrong to raise doubts or to stir up controversy from the pulpit. My duty was to strengthen faith, and to nurture the spiritual life of my flock. I tried to avoid making statements that might undermine deeply-held convictions.

Derek: There are still some Christians who think it wrong to question anything. Isn't there a hymn which says: 'To doubt would be disloyalty, To falter would be sin'?

Arthur: That's Frederick Faber, if I'm not mistaken. But the doubt he is referring to relates to the belief that 'right is right, since God is God, And right the day must win' (1). That is surely basic to our Christian commitment. There may be issues we are justified in retaining an open mind about, but that is not one of them!

Gillian: Then should we distinguish between things we can agree to differ about, and things which are so central we should never question them?

Arthur: Well, we are all committed to the service of God as revealed in Christ - at least, I assume we are. The church is not a debating society for the consideration of interesting ideas.

Derek: Fred Pratt Green's hymn suggests that doubt can lead to a more mature faith. Do you agree with that idea, Arthur?

Arthur: Doubt can have that effect, certainly. It may be an indication that the Spirit of Truth is at work within us. I believe that has been my own experience, although how mature I have become I'll leave others to judge! But doubt can also have a destructive effect. If it weakens your trust in God it is hardly leading you towards maturity. I've often considered the cry of Job in the midst of his troubles: 'Though he slay me, yet will I trust in him' (2). That's the faith we need.

Frank: Earlier on you mentioned Auschwitz and Hiroshima. Excuse me for going back to this, but I'm often ten minutes behind the rest of the group! I was wondering if you have any light to throw on this problem. You must have thought a good deal about it.

Arthur: I've found it helpful to think of God sharing in the suffering. I first came across this idea in the poems of Studdert-Kennedy. He had been a padre on the Western Front during the First World War, and he had seen some terrible suffering. He came to believe God *must* be affected by this; any other conception of God was unacceptable.

I also believe God is able to *redeem* suffering, although how he does this I am unable to explain. It is not easy to see how the suffering of a severely handicapped child can be redeemed, or the wretchedness of starving families in Africa. But the basic pattern in the life of the world is death and resurrection. I believe this may reflect a rhythm in the life of God himself. But who can say? The being of God will always remain a mystery to us.

Derek: We're coming towards the end of our time. You've given us a great deal to think about, Arthur, and we're very grateful to you. Is there any other point one of you would like to raise?

Marion: You must have had to deal with a large number of people during your ministry. Have you ever been tempted to despair of human nature?

Arthur: I have been disappointed on occasions. People do not always live up to your expectation of them! I have felt frustrated by some people's stubbornness. But I've never reached the point of thinking: 'What's the use? There's nothing to be done with these folk.' God works in surprising ways. His light and grace have often been displayed in unexpected places.

Derek: That would be a fitting place at which to end. Thank you again, Arthur, for all your help.

(1) 'Workman of God! O lose not heart' (H&Ps 489)

(2) Job 13 v.15

Comment

The final sentence of one of Professor Herbert Butterfield's books has become justly famous: 'Hold to Christ, and for the rest be totally uncommitted' (*Christianity and History*, Fontana edition 1957, p.189). In the last resort truth is embodied not in a set of propositions but in a Person. The Creator and Sustainer of all things has revealed his nature and purpose in the Christ-event - in the life, death, resurrection, and proclamation of Jesus of Nazareth. Therein lies the heart of our faith.

There was another informal committee meeting after this session of the Thursday Group for anyone who wished to stay. Somebody asked about further reading. Derek commented that he still found William Barclay's *The Plan Man Looks at the Apostles' Creed* (Fontana 1967) helpful, but that it might not appeal to everyone. The best course was to seek answers to specific questions, using local libraries and Christian bookshops to make one's own discoveries.

Topics for the following year were also discussed, but it is time for us to take our leave of the Church of the Good Shepherd at Barfield and return to the company of our own fellow-pilgrims.